Handbook of
T'ai Chi Ch'uan Exercises

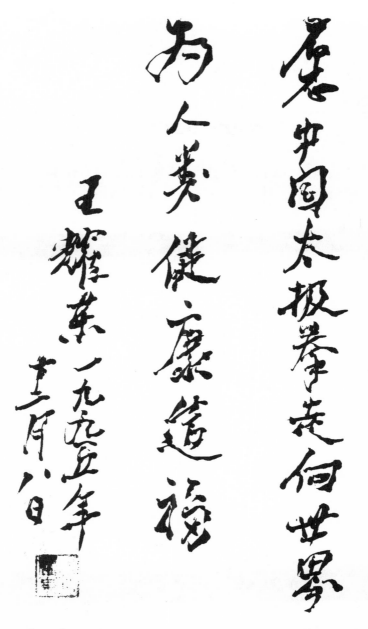

願中國太极拳走向世界

为人美健康造福

王耀東 一九九五年 十二月八日

The above inscription was written specially for this book by 96-year-old Professor Wang Yaodong on December 8, 1995. It says: "May China's T'ai Chi Ch'uan spread all over the world to benefit human health!"

Handbook of
T'ai Chi Ch'uan
Exercises

Zhang Fuxing

WEISER BOOKS
Boston, MA/York Beach, ME

First published in 1996 by
Red Wheel/Weiser, LLC
368 Congress Street
Boston, MA 02210

Library of Congress Cataloging-in-Publication Data

Zhang, Fuxing
    Handbook of T'ai Chi Ch'uan Exercises / Zhang Fuxing.
        p.   cm.
    Includes index.
    ISBN 0-87728-891-7 (alk. paper)
    1. T'ai Chi Ch'uan. I. Title.
  GV504.Z53   1996
  613.7'148—dc20   96-8713

Printed in the United States of America
VG

08 07 06 05 04
10 9 8 7 6 5 4

Typeset in 12 pt. Veljovic Book

The paper used in this publication meets the minimum requirements of the American National Standard for Information Sciences—Permanence of Paper for Printed Library Materials Z39.48-1992(R1997).

T'ai Chi Ch'uan

An Internal Form of Chinese Boxing
An Ancient and Unique Fitness Art

T'ai Chi Ch'uan can:
- improve circulation;
- promote digestion;
- increase coordination;
- heighten awareness;
- help lose weight properly;
- make joints stronger, more elastic and flexible;
- improve physical, mental and emotional health;
- increase the immune function and prevent illness;
- slow the aging process and prolong your life.

Whether you are young or old, weak or strong, so long as you learn and practice it daily, you will certainly be able to derive benefits from it.

Unlike other martial arts, T'ai Chi avoids use of external strength. You are just asked to combine slow, deep abdominal breathing with gentle, smooth body movements in a natural way.

No special equipment is needed to practice T'ai Chi; it can be performed anywhere, even in a small room.

Make T'ai Chi practice a part of your daily life, and that will lead the way to super health and longevity.

Table of Contents

Preface

I have studied and practiced T'ai Chi Ch'uan for over forty years. It helped me overcome several chronic and stubborn diseases (including gastric ulcer, neurasthenia, hepatomegaly, and heart disease), and enabled me to live a healthy life. Practicing T'ai Chi daily gives me renewed strength and vitality. I believe that, owing to my perseverance in practicing this ancient fitness art, I can live longer in good health. I always hope to share its benefit and my experience with others; hence this handbook.

I feel delighted as well as honored to be able to introduce to English readers the complete set of T'ai Chi Ch'uan developed by the Sports Committee of the People's Republic of China. It goes without saying that the handbook contains my personal experiences and insights. I have laid stress on practice, on how to handle every posture and movement, and on T'ai Chi Ch'uan's basic essentials.

It would have been impossible for me to complete the work without the help of my teachers, my friends, and my family members. I am very much obliged to my beloved teacher, 96-year-old Professor Wang Yaodong, for his instruction and encouragement, and particularly for his precious photographs and the inscription he has specially done for this handbook (see frontispiece). I also want to express my heartfelt gratitude to 91-year-old teacher, Professor Ai Zigao, who, as an expert of T'ai Chi Ch'uan, has helped me clarify some questionable points relating to the art.

I also owe much to my wife, Wang Duafang, for her full support and understanding; to my son-in-law, Wang Wuyi, for inspiring me and taking pictures for the book; to my son-in-law, Zhou Qing, who has painstakingly taken photos and made a videotape for me; and to all my children for their support and inspiration, especially my son Zhang Daxian and daughter Zhang Wailu, who have done a great deal of work for me. I am also particularly grateful to Ms. Diane Swedin for her enthusiastic support and cheerful help. She is an experienced practitioner of T'ai Chi Ch'uan, and what is more, knows well the ancient Chinese civilization, especially the Yi Ching and Taoism. I would also like to express my sincere thanks to everyone who has supported and helped me.

Finally, I want to say that it will be the greatest pleasure and the highest reward for my work if this handbook can play a positive role in improving your health, promoting your happiness, and increasing your lifespan.

My Teachers and T'ai Chi Ch'uan

Professor Wang Yaodong

My teacher, Professor Wang Yaodong, was born in 1900. He has been engaged in the teaching and research of physical culture (including the art of T'ai Chi Ch'uan) since he graduated from Peking Teachers University in 1922. As a famous professor of Physical Culture, he taught early or late at Peking University, Peking Teachers University, and Northwestern University for over seventy years. He has written many works concerning physical training and instruction. He acted as Vice Chairman of the All-China General Association of Physical Culture for many years, and is still an Honorary Committee Member of that organization. In 1984, as a member of the Chinese Physical Culture Visiting Group, he came to Los Angeles to view the 23rd Olympic Games, and at the same time he visited several big cities in this country. He, himself, persists in T'ai Chi practice every day.

More than fifty years ago, when I was a student at Northwestern University, I received physical education from Professor Wang Yaodong every week. Not long after I had finished my studies, I became a teacher at another university. Unfortunately, I suffered from stomach trouble and neurosis, and my health was so bad that I could hardly get on with my work. I felt very worried. One day, I went to my old school to visit Professor Wang. At hearing that I was troubled with those illnesses, he advised me to learn and practice T'ai Chi Ch'uan. I accepted his advice, and began to learn T'ai Chi Ch'uan from him. I learned and practiced it earnestly, day after day, month after month. With the lapse of time, my health got better and better, and my diseases were dispelled gradually. I became aware of the benefits of

Wild Horse Waves its Mane (right).

Wild Horse Waves its Mane (left).

Professor Wang Yaodong
At ninety-six years he is an inspiration.

T'ai Chi Ch'uan, and was determined to continue with T'ai Chi training. This enabled me to live a healthy life.

Professor Ai Zigao

Born in 1905, Professor Ai Zigao is an old colleague, as well as a teacher of mine. He, as a professor of Physical Culture, and I, as a professor of Translation, worked and lived in the same school, Xi'an Foreign Languages University, for several decades. And, as he is also an expert of T'ai Chi Ch'uan, I frequently consult him on questions relating to the art of T'ai Chi Ch'uan, so I always consider him as my teacher.

Daily Practice

T'ai Chi practice has become an indispensable part of my daily life. Whenever I fail to do it, I lose my appetite and don't feel as energetic as usual. I am now 76 years old and I practice T'ai Chi outside early every morning. Sometimes I also practice it in the evening before going to bed. I often do the exercise in a nearby park or playground, or in a quiet place with fresh air. If it is raining, snowing, or blowing hard, I do my practice inside the house. Usually, I practice a whole set of Standard T'ai Chi Ch'uan each day for about 25 minutes. Each time I finish my performance, I feel relaxed, comfortable, full of energy, and can walk with brisk and stable steps. The following photographs show me practicing certain postures of T'ai Chi Ch'uan. Hopefully, these photographs will inspire people of all ages to try this helpful art.

Single Whip.

White Crane Spreads His Wings.

Brush Knee and Twist Step.

Play "Pipa."

Needle at Sea Bottom.

Fend off and Push Away.

Sway Body to Subdue the Tiger.

Wild Horse Waves Its Mane.

Golden Cock Stands on One Leg.

Step Back to Mount the Tiger.

CHAPTER I

Introductory Remarks

T'ai Chi Ch'uan, an internal form of Chinese boxing, has been practiced by millions of Chinese people for many centuries. Formerly, people learned it for self-defense; now, it serves as a mass fitness art to be learned and practiced for improving health and dispelling illness.

As a soft traditional Chinese martial art and an exquisite slow exercise that is beneficial for both men and women, old and young, it is ever prevailing in China's cities and towns. You cannot help but notice T'ai Chi's enormous devotees and enthusiasts when you visit China; especially during the early morning, everywhere—in parks, playgrounds, courtyards and even on roadside spaces and building rooftops, you can see people in large or small groups absorbed in T'ai Chi practice. It has won a high reputation, not only in China, but also in most parts of the world for its various benefits to health.

1. The Origin and Philosophy of T'ai Chi Ch'uan

What is meant by "T'ai Chi"? It literally means "Supreme Ultimate." In the view of China's ancient philosophers, it represents the primary cause of the existence of the universe, and possesses a soft and tranquil quality. What is meant by "Ch'uan"? The Chinese "Ch'uan," according to its literal meaning, is equal to "fist" in English terms, but here it does not indicate "fist," it signifies "Boxing" or "Martial Art."

People in the ancient Chinese city, Xi'an,
practicing T'ai Chi Ch'uan in the early morning.

Therefore, T'ai Chi Ch'uan may be translated as "Supreme Ultimate Boxing," or "Supreme Ultimate Martial Art."

The concept of "T'ai Chi" originates from the Yi Ching, China's oldest philosophy book, known as *The Book of Changes* in English. It holds that all universal beings, and even the universe itself, are composed of two elements (or forces) represented by Yin and Yang. Yin refers to the element (or force) which is negative, female. Yang stands for the element (or force) which is positive, male. The Yin element (or force) produces darkness, coldness, softness, and emptiness. The Yang element (or force) generates light, warmth, hardness, and fullness. Although Yin and Yang represent two opposites, they reside together, interact with each other, and unite as one, just like the T'ai Chi symbol, also called the Yin-Yang symbol or the "Double Fish" diagram.

Yin and Yang contradict as well as complement each other, and create all things by way of their interaction. This signifies that every object has positive and negative elements

T'ai Chi Symbol.
(The black represents Yin, and the white Yang.)

within itself; that is to say, there is Yin in Yang, and Yang in Yin. Yin-Yang opposites unite. This is the law of nature followed by the Taoist school.

The philosophy of T'ai Chi Ch'uan is mainly based on the Yin-Yang theory and Taoism. Taoism, as a school of thought, advocates that people should identify themselves with the spirit of nature, and believes that "the weak overcome the strong; the gentle overcome the violent." "The hard and powerful will disintegrate; the soft and yielding will prevail." The Taoists often use water as example, saying that "there is nothing more soft and yielding than water, yet nothing can equal water's strength." Therefore, T'ai Chi Ch'uan emphasizes "softness."

Tradition has it that an early Taoist priest, named Chang San-feng, founded the art of T'ai Chi Ch'uan in conformity with Taoist philosophy and the Yin-Yang theory. As it has been told, Chang made it clear that T'ai Chi Ch'uan was not created for the purpose of fighting. It was aimed at building up the body and prolonging life. Chang is a figure full of legendary color in China's history. He was depicted as an eccentric person with huge eyes and a heavy beard, care-

Taoist Priest Chang San-feng,
the founder of T'ai Chi Ch'uan.

less about his own appearance, always looking cheerful, and
constantly wearing the same garment and straw hat whether
it was winter or summer. He is believed to have lived for
several hundred years. The dates of his birth and death are
unknown, and even which dynasty (Song, Yuan, or Ming)
he belonged to still remains uncertain.

2. The Schools of T'ai Chi Ch'uan

T'ai Chi Ch'uan is one of China's greatest gifts to mankind. It
has sparked wide interest both inside and outside China. Like
other arts, however, during its long and tortuous development,
T'ai Chi Ch'uan has divided into several different schools, such
as the Chen style, the Yang style, the Wú (its Chinese symbol
is 吴) style, the Wǔ (its Chinese symbol is 武) style, and the Sun
style. Each of them has its own features. And yet among them
the most popular is the Yang style.

The Yang style was founded by Master Yang Fu-kui, also known as Yang Lu-chan, who originally was a student of Master Chen Chang-xing, the founder of the Chen style, and afterwards developed from the Chen family his own style, the Yang style. This style is characterized by its softness, slowness, gentleness, steadiness, and its smooth, harmonious and graceful movements. This style has only a history of about 150 years, yet it has already spread throughout the world, and is practiced by more and more people.

What is presented in this handbook is a set of T'ai Chi Ch'uan belonging to the Yang school. This set of T'ai Chi Ch'uan was developed by the Sports Committee of the People's Republic of China on the basis of the traditional Yang style during the 1950's, in order to meet the needs of the people who were interested in this kind of setting-up exercise. This set of T'ai Chi Ch'uan, acclaimed as "Peking form," emphasizes maintaining and improving health, rather than self-defense. This set of T'ai Chi Ch'uan still retains all the characteristics of the Yang style, but is relatively easy to learn and master. It is especially fit for middle-aged and old people to learn and practice. It has fully proved to be beneficial to health and longevity, and has been well received by the general public.

3. *The Physical Benefits of T'ai Chi Ch'uan*

T'ai Chi Ch'uan is an all-sided exercise, which not only builds up one's limbs and trunk through various movements, but also strengthens one's inner organs and central nervous system by wielding slow, deep abdominal breathing and concentrating one's thought. It is considered, and has proved to be, a good healing and health-promoting exercise. It produces both physical and mental effects on preventing and dispelling illness. In China, T'ai Chi Ch'uan has been applied as a supplementary means in many hospitals and sanitariums, wherein some patients are taught the exercise to help them cure their sickness or speed their recovery.

Why can T'ai Chi Ch'uan prevent and cure illness? According to the Yin-Yang theory and traditional Chinese medicine, the reason why we fall ill is because we have lost the harmony and balance of Yin and Yang. One of T'ai Chi Ch'uan's most important effects is the ability to coordinate one's Yin and Yang, keeping the total being in a condition of dynamic equilibrium, both physically and psychologically. Perhaps this may be considered as a general answer to the question.

In recent years, many medical research institutes in China made various scientific researches and experiments on the healing and health-giving effects of T'ai Chi Ch'uan. The results of the research show that many diseases, such as heart disease, high blood pressure, gastric ulcer, and other stomach troubles, neurasthenia, and other nervous disorders, consumption, and other respiratory ailments, arthritis, and many other chronic illnesses, can be cured or alleviated through the regular and longterm practice of T'ai Chi Ch'uan.

Researchers found that most of the T'ai Chi practitioners have a low heart rate and low blood pressure, and that their blood circulation is distinctly improved during practice.

Researchers found that the digestive system is greatly affected by T'ai Chi training. This is because T'ai Chi practice is matched with slow, deep abdominal breathing, which causes the internal organs to be massaged, and promotes the movement of food through the stomach and intestines, thus making digestion and assimilation of food more effective. As a matter of fact, those who practice T'ai Chi Ch'uan daily all have a good appetite.

Researchers found that T'ai Chi practice is extremely beneficial to the nervous system. This is because the high degree of concentration of mind in T'ai Chi practice strengthens the central nervous system and stimulates the cerebral cortex, thus helping the brain rest and relieve certain nervous and mental diseases.

Researchers also discovered that T'ai Chi practice has a positive effect on increasing the immune system, and on slowing the aging process.

In addition, T'ai Chi Ch'uan has proved to be an effective approach to help overweight people, through perseverance, lose their weight properly and better their physical condition. Moreover, T'ai Chi's low stances, slow and continuous movements, and constant shifting of weight can help older people increase their ability to keep balance and avoid falls.

As an internal martial art, T'ai Chi Ch'uan emphasizes relaxation, softness, and inner quiet. People find that T'ai Chi practice creates an overall sense of well-being.

Again, many postures of T'ai Chi Ch'uan have wonderful and poetic names, such as "White Crane Spreads Its Wings," "Wild Horse Waves Its Mane," "Golden Cock Stands on One Leg," "Fair Lady Works with Shuttles," "Carry Tiger to Mountain," "White Snake Puts Out Its Tongue," etc. These give a clear idea of what one is expected to do. Yes, during practice, one must try to imitate some movements and postures of Nature. This is very interesting; most people enjoy it!

There are some essentials and basic rules of vital importance to T'ai Chi Ch'uan which must be understood and strictly observed in practice. They are common to all styles. The next two chapters will outline them.

CHAPTER II

Four Major Characteristics of T'ai Chi Ch'uan

T'ai Chi Ch'uan is a martial art peculiar to the Chinese nation. It is different from any other martial arts or physical exercises. By comparison it has at least four major characteristics. They are as follows:

1. Softness, Gentleness, and Slowness

As a martial art, T'ai Chi Ch'uan emphasizes cultivating internal energies. It avoids use of external strength, especially awkward strength. It is soft and gentle. All movements should be carried on in a smooth, slow, and steady way. There is no allowance for any violent or jumping actions and sudden changes of rising and falling. At the conclusion of a performance, you may be dripping with sweat, but there will be no shortness of breath; you will not feel tired, but rather will feel relaxed and comfortable. Because of this, T'ai Chi Ch'uan is considered to be an ideal keep-fit exercise suitable for anyone, regardless of age, sex, or constitution, particularly for those in delicate health or with chronic diseases. However, it must be pointed out that T'ai Chi Ch'uan looks soft, but there is hardness concealed inside the softness. It is often likened to "steel wrapped in cotton."

2. Continuity and Evenness

Another cardinal characteristic of T'ai Chi Ch'uan is its continuity and evenness. In spite of its complicated movements

and changeful postures, T'ai Chi Ch'uan demands practitioners perform it from the "Starting Posture" to the "Concluding Posture" in a continued and uninterrupted way, and at
an even and unhurried speed, like floating clouds and flow-
ing water, without any breaks or junctions between two
movements or postures.

3. *Circularity*

The third characteristic of T'ai Chi Ch'uan is its circularity.
T'ai Chi Ch'uan distinguishes itself from other martial arts
by its unique movements. It demands all movements of the
upper limbs to go in circles, which may be plane or vertical,
big or small, in an ellipse or a semicircle. So it is called a
form of "round exercises." The reason why every movement
contains a circle is that circular movements are conducive
to healthy developments of the body's various parts, since
they conform with the natural motion of the body's joints.
Besides, it is said that, by adopting circular movements, one
may neutralize or divert the force of a coming attack, and
make the opponent lose the center of gravity. Therefore,
when you are practicing, your arms, no matter in what direction they move, should always go in a round or arc-like
way. They should never move along a straight line. The arms
themselves are also required to bend a little, to be kept in
an arc-shape.

4. *Wholeness and Harmony*

The fourth characteristic is its wholeness and harmony. Once
you begin practicing T'ai Chi Ch'uan, your whole body, including all parts and internal organs, will immediately enter a moving state, and your torso and four limbs, as well as
your mind and breath, are required to act in close coordination. At no time will your upper limbs be in action while
the lower ones remain still, or vice versa.

During the whole process of practice, your waist always plays a dominating role. The actions of your body pivot on your waist (strictly speaking, on the lumbar vertebra), that is to say, it is your waist that brings your arms, legs, and all other parts together into action. As your body changes direction and position, it will move without division, slowly and unceasingly until your performance comes to an end.

CHAPTER III

Some Key Points of Practice

The following fundamentals of T'ai Chi Ch'uan are of great importance to practitioners. In order to embody T'ai Chi Ch'uan's characteristics outlined in the last chapter, to learn the art well, and to acquire an ideal effect, you must try your best to understand and master these fundamentals through daily practice.

1. Mind Leading Movements

In the whole course of performing T'ai Chi Ch'uan, all the body movements should be carried on under the conscious direction of your mind. Before you begin to move, make sure you know what you are going to do. For instance, if you are going to practice "White Crane Spreads Its Wings," you should have an image of that posture in your mind before you actually do it. Your mind is like a thread running through all of your movements, leading and dominating every action. As the saying goes, "Your mind is the commander, your body must follow your mind." To have a good grasp of this concept, you must try to fulfill the following two points:

A. Make yourself as quiet and calm as possible before you begin practice.
B. Rid your mind of all extraneous thoughts, and concentrate on how to perform the art.

2. Pay Attention to Relaxation

The key to a successful and effective practice of T'ai Chi Ch'uan lies in relaxation. You must pay special attention to keeping your whole body in a relaxed (though not lax or limp) state, both physically and mentally, during the whole process. Whether or not you can achieve a real and proper relaxation depends on whether or not you can correctly fulfill the requirements for various parts of the body.

What are the requirements? According to the classics of T'ai Chi Ch'uan, when engaging the practice, the shoulders should be sunk, the elbows drooped (meaning the arms should not be straightened), the chest held in, not protruding, the back slightly rounded, the torso erect in its natural form (not leaning forward or backward, right or left), and the head slightly raised as if suspended from its top. If you want to enter a real state of relaxation, you must comply with these requirements.

Relaxation and correct form are interdependent and supplement each other. If your form is really correct, you will be easily relaxed, and if you are really relaxed, your form will be more correct. Again, you must relax the whole body as well as the mind, eliminating tension and allowing the body's bones and muscles, internal organs, blood vessels and nerves to reach a natural and comfortable state. Also, before practice, you should loosen your belt and any other restrictive clothing.

3. Coordinate the Actions of Arms, Legs, and Torso

Why does T'ai Chi Ch'uan put so much emphasis on coordination? It is because T'ai Chi Ch'uan is a form of exercise intended to exert training on the practitioner's whole body, not just a certain part. Such a purpose of overall training can only be attained through a series of concerted actions of the torso and four limbs. Therefore, during the practice of T'ai Chi Ch'uan, you must be aware of all your parts and coordinate them well in order to reach a perfect alignment of the whole person.

The moves of T'ai Chi Ch'uan look relatively simple, yet coordinating the movements of the upper and lower limbs, as well as the other parts of the body, is not so easy as it may appear. Because of this, you had better not do the complete form all at once in the beginning; you may repeatedly practice a few postures, such as the "Starting Posture," "Wild Horse Waves Its Mane," "White Crane Spreads Its Wings," "Wave Hands like Clouds," etc. Through this you can practice coordination of your torso and four limbs, and also practice shifting your weight and changing your steps. In the meantime, you can also learn and master some footwork, such as "horse-riding stance," "bow-shaped step," "empty step," etc.

4. Master the Center of Gravity and Distinguish between "Emptiness" and "Fullness"

According to the rules of T'ai Chi Ch'uan, most of your weight should always be on one of your legs during practice. The leg that is bearing most of your weight is called a "full leg," and the other one an "empty leg." The "empty leg" (or "empty foot"), usually called "empty step" in terms of martial art, is not absolutely powerless. It still plays a role of fulcrum, maintaining the body's balance.

If your weight is distributed evenly on both of your legs, both of them will become "full legs." This state, to use a traditional expression, is called "double weighting," which is regarded as a "taboo" to T'ai Chi Ch'uan, and thus should be avoided except in the "Starting Posture," "Concluding Posture," and "Cross Hands."

Distinction between "emptiness" and "fullness" is directly affected by the shifting of weight. During the practice of T'ai Chi Ch'uan, you are constantly required to shift your weight front or back, left or right. No matter in what direction your weight is shifted, you must try your best to shift it appropriately. Practice shows that an overdone shifting of weight will cause unbalance; an inadequate shifting of weight will bring about "double weighting," and make the distinction between "emptiness" and "fullness" impossible. Without good balance, without clear distinction between "emptiness" and "fullness," it is impossible to move with stable and skillful steps.

In order to explain how to shift weight just right, namely how to master the center of gravity, and how to distinguish "emptiness" and "fullness" clearly, an example is given as follows:

If you are going to perform a left "bow-shaped step," you should first take a step forward with your left leg, then gradually shift your weight forward onto your left leg until your left knee bends to such a degree that it is just over the tiptoe of your left foot, that is to say, the knee and tiptoe are just in a vertical line. If the knee protrudes beyond the tiptoe, that means the shifting of weight is overdone; if the knee fails to reach that place, that means the shifting of weight is inadequate. Now, your left leg (the one carrying most of your weight) is "full," and your right leg is "empty." Then again, suppose you are asked to change the left "bow-shaped step" into a left "empty step." You should gradually shift your weight backward onto your right leg until your right knee bends to such a degree that it is just over the tiptoe of your right foot. Now, your right leg becomes "full," and your left leg becomes "empty."

Remember, only when you deal with your weight, your center of gravity, properly, can a clear distinction between "emptiness" and "fullness" be achieved, and only when you distinguish between "emptiness" and "fullness" clearly, can you maintain good balance and assure calm, even, and agile movements of your arms and legs.

5. Let Breath Follow Movement Naturally

T'ai Chi Ch'uan demands the practitioner breathe naturally. In practicing T'ai Chi Ch'uan, your breath should not be obstructed by your movements, nor should your movements be restrained by your breath.

This does not mean, however, that you may be neglectful of your breath while practicing. As is known to all, T'ai Chi Ch'uan is essentially a kind of "qigong." Chinese qigong is generally practiced in two major categories: "still" and "moving." "Still" qigong lays emphasis on quiet, motionless meditation. "Moving" qigong involves movements of the limbs and body. T'ai Chi Ch'uan is considered to be the best "moving" qigong, a meditation in motion. Therefore, in the practice of T'ai Chi Ch'uan, proper breathing exercises are absolutely necessary. Without breathing exercises, T'ai Chi Ch'uan will lose its most important feature and be undifferentiated from other physical activities; without breathing exercises, no obvious keep-fit and therapeutic effects can be obtained. But any arbitrary breathing exercises are not to be tolerated.

T'ai Chi Ch'uan emphasizes natural abdominal breathing. What is called natural abdominal breathing is inhaling by gently expanding the abdomen, and exhaling by slowly contracting the abdominal muscles. Only through slow, deep abdominal breathing can your practice bring about ideal effects. But you must change your breath naturally. Never force it to fit into your movement. If you attempt to match your breath with your movements artificially, you will very likely do yourself harm.

There are some general rules about breathing, such as: while the hand-arm movements are going upward, backward or inward, you are asked to inhale with tongue touching your upper palate; while the hand-arm movements are going downward, forward, or outward, you are asked to exhale with your tongue resting on lower palate; while your arms are moving in opposite directions, your breath should follow one of your arms that accords with your breath. It is not advisable, however, for a beginner to attempt this. It is only after you have been able to practice every posture skillfully that you may allow your breath and movements to match with each other naturally according to the rules.

In order to avoid side-effects, it is better to do the breathing exercises under the direction of an experienced teacher, especially during the beginning stage.

Breathing is closely related to form and relaxation. When your body is relaxed, your breath will become easier; and when you are performing the movements correctly, your breath will change naturally of its own accord.

6. Even Speed and Even Height

It is a taboo to practice T'ai Chi Ch'uan at a faster speed one moment and at a slower speed the next. So you must try your best to keep your performance at an even speed from the first posture to the last one. Meanwhile, T'ai Chi Ch'uan should be done at a slow speed rather than a fast one. Through slow practice you can lay a solid foundation and achieve good results. At a normal speed, the "Simplified T'ai Chi Ch'uan" takes 5 to 6 minutes (or 7 to 8 minutes if you do it at a somewhat slower speed), and the "Standard T'ai Chi Ch'uan" takes about 20 minutes, or a bit longer.

It is also a taboo to practice T'ai Chi Ch'uan at varying levels of height. You should fix the height of the form (namely the degree to which the knee is bent) at the very beginning (in the "Starting Posture") and hold it throughout the entire performance (except for the posture of "Squat Down"). The form may be higher or lower. It is advisable for beginners, older people, as well as those with a weak physical condition to adopt the higher form. Once their movements become skillful, and their physical strength has increased through consistent training, they may gradually adjust themselves to the lower form.

7. *Gradual Development*

In learning T'ai Chi Ch'uan, you should proceed in an orderly way and step-by-step; never act in haste. More haste, less speed. Not only should T'ai Chi Ch'uan be performed slowly, but it also should be learned slowly. Only by slow learning can you catch the pith and marrow of the art, and become one with posture and form.

Remember, there are no pills which will transform the beginner into a capable T'ai Chi Ch'uan practitioner overnight. It is vital to realize that you must practice according to your body's ability and strength. Those of you with chronic diseases should never strive anxiously for quick results.

8. *Patience, Endurance, and Perseverance*

As has been stated above, T'ai Chi Ch'uan is quite different from any other physical exercises. It sets strict demands, not only on the various parts of the body, but on one's breath and mind. It is really not very easy to master. If you want to be successful in your practice, you must provide yourself with patience, endurance, and perseverance.

Perseverance is particularly important. You are required to practice daily. You are required to persist in your practice many months, many years, and even all your life. The longer you can persevere, the more you will benefit. If you practice by fits and starts, you will never come to know T'ai Chi Ch'uan.

Remember, learning and practicing T'ai Ch Ch'uan calls for your patience, endurance, and perseverance, and in turn will build your patience, endurance, and perseverance.

With this knowledge, let us begin our journey. You have my hand, and I have yours.

CHAPTER IV

Simplified T'ai Chi Ch'uan

During the 1950s, the Sports Committee of the People's Republic of China, having widely solicited opinions from T'ai Chi Ch'uan experts, developed a short form and a long form of T'ai Chi Ch'uan based on the traditional Yang style. The short form is usually called Simplified T'ai Chi Ch'uan, and the long form is usually called Standard T'ai Chi Ch'uan (See chapter V). They plus Push Hands form a complete set of authentic "T'ai Chi Ch'uan Exercises" and have been prevailing in China ever since.

The short form has only 24 postures, and is easy to learn and master, yet it has the same therapeutic and keep-fit value as the long form. Its postures and component movements are described and illustrated one by one, step by step, as follows:

1. Starting Posture

Movement 1: Stand erect with both feet parallel and shoulder-width apart. Let your arms hang down naturally. Relax your chest muscles. Slightly hold in your lower jaw. Concentrate your mind. Look horizontally forward (see fig. 1).

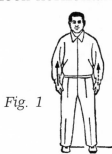

Fig. 1

Movement 2: Slowly raise your arms in front of you with palms facing down, until your hands reach shoulder-height. Keep the distance between your hands a shoulder-width apart (see figs. 2, 3).

Fig. 2

Fig. 3

Movement 3: Keep your upper body upright. Bend your knees slightly and squat down gently. While doing so, your arms slowly descend with elbows drooping and vertically opposite the knees. Eyes look straight ahead (see fig. 4).

Fig. 4

Notes:

A. In this posture, your weight should be distributed evenly on both feet.

B. The lowering of your arms should be in harmony with the bending of your knees.

C. Keep your shoulders sunk, elbows drooped, and fingers slightly curled.

D. Do not throw out your buttocks while squatting down.

2. *Wild Horse Waves Its Mane (Left and Right)*

Movement 1 (continued from fig. 4): Turn your body slightly to the right, shift your weight onto your right foot and bring your left foot close to the right, toes on the ground. While doing so, your right hand goes up and backward to rest in front of your chest, palm down, fingers separated and curved; your left hand travels down and right to lie just below the right, palm up, fingers separated and curved. Now, your hands look as if they were holding a big ball, and your eyes look at your right hand (see figs. 5, 6).

Fig. 5   *Fig. 6*

Movement 2: Turn your upper body to the left with the right toes moving slightly inward, then take a step to the left with your left foot, and shift your weight onto it, forming a left "bow-shaped step" (it is usually called "forward lunge" in martial arts). While shifting your weight, your hands go apart—the left hand moving left and up to eye-height, palm inclined upward, and the right hand falling down to the side of your right hip with palm facing down. Eyes now look at left palm (see figs. 7, 8, 9).

Fig. 7   *Fig. 8*   *Fig. 9*

Movement 3: Shift your weight backward onto your right foot, turn your left toes slightly outward, and, in pace with this, turn your body left and shift your weight onto your left foot again. At the same time, bring your left hand backward to lie in front of your chest, palm down, and let your right hand move left in a curve to rest below the left, palm up, so that your two hands form a holding-ball position; meanwhile, draw your right foot close to the left, toes on the ground. Eyes now look at the left hand (see figs. 10, 11, 12).

Fig. 10   *Fig. 11*   *Fig. 12*

Movement 4: Now take a step to the right with your right foot and shift your weight onto it, forming a right bow-shaped step. Meanwhile, raise your right hand in a curve to eye level with palm facing slantingly upward, and lower your left hand to the side of your left hip with palm facing down. Eyes now look at the right palm (see figs. 13, 14).

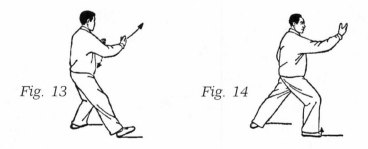

Fig. 13   *Fig. 14*

Movement 5: Practice according to the explanation of Movement 3, but with opposite hands and feet (see figs. 15, 16, 17).

Fig. 15 *Fig. 16* *Fig. 17*

Movement 6: Practice according to the explanation of Movement 4, but with opposite hands and feet (see figs. 18, 19).

Fig. 18 *Fig. 19*

Notes:

A. Your upper body should be kept erect, not leaning forward or backward, left or right, and its turning should always pivot on your waist.

B. Your chest should be fully relaxed, and your arms should assume an arc-like fashion when your hands go apart from each other.

C. The parting of hands and the forming of a bow-shaped step should be done in a coordinated way and at an even pace.

D. In forming a bow-shaped step, do not bend your knee beyond the toes of the foot.

3. White Crane Spreads Its Wings

Movement 1 (continued from fig. 19): Turn your upper body slightly to the left, draw your left hand back in front of your chest, palm down, and turn your right hand over (palm up), bringing it across your waist in a curve to form a holding-ball position with the left hand (see fig. 20).

Fig. 20

Movement 2: Let your right foot take a half step forward, gently draw your upper body back so as to shift your weight onto the right leg; then move your left leg a little forward with the toes touching the ground, forming a left empty step. In the meantime, raise your right hand in front of you to the right side of your head, palm inward, and lower your left hand to the side of your left hip, palm down. Eyes now look forward (see figs. 21, 22).

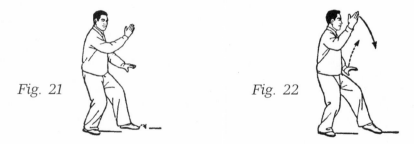

Fig. 21   *Fig. 22*

Notes:

A. Do not throw out your chest and square your shoulders at the end of the posture.

B. Keep your left knee slightly bent and your arms in an arc-shape.

4. Brush Knee and Twist Step (Left and Right)

Movement 1 (continued from fig. 22): Lower your right hand in front of your body, then let it go back and up, in a curve, to ear level, palm facing up, and bring your left hand right and up in a curve, to the right side of your chest, palm facing down. At the same time, turn your upper body to the right. Eyes now look at right hand (see figs. 23, 24, 25).

Fig. 23   Fig. 24   Fig. 25

Movement 2: Turn your upper body left, take a step forward to the left with the left foot, and shift your weight onto it, forming a left bow-shaped step. Meanwhile, bring your right hand back from behind and push it forward by the side of your right ear, keeping it at nose level, palm outward; let your left hand go down and brush past your left knee to rest beside your left hip. Eyes now look at the forefinger of right hand (see figs. 26, 27).

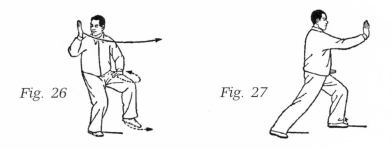

Fig. 26   Fig. 27

Movement 3: Gently draw your upper body back and bend your right leg so as to shift your weight onto it. Turn your left toes slightly outward, and turn your body left at the same time. Then bend your left leg to assume a bow-shaped step, and move your right foot close to the left with heel raised and toes touching the ground. In company with the movements of your lower limbs, your left hand turns over (palm up) and moves backward and upward to ear level, palm facing up; your right hand, with the turning of your body, comes back in front of your left shoulder with palm facing down. Eyes now look at the left hand (see figs. 28, 29, 30).

Fig. 28   Fig. 29   Fig. 30

Movement 4: Practice according to the explanation of Movement 2, but with opposite hands and feet (see figs. 31, 32).

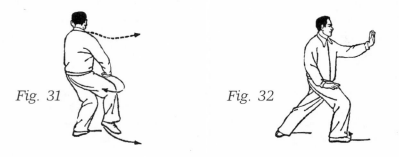

Fig. 31   Fig. 32

Movement 5: Practice according to the explanation of Movement 3, but with opposite hands and feet (see figs. 33, 34, 35).

Fig. 33   Fig. 34

Fig. 35

Movement 6: Repeat Movement 2 (see figs. 36, 37).

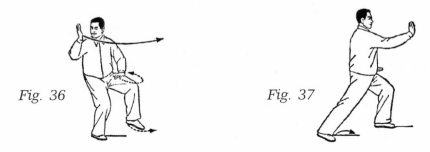

Fig. 36   Fig. 37

Notes:

A. While pushing your hand forward or moving it backward, keep your upper body erect, droop your shoulder and elbow, and relax your waist and hips.

B. Pushing hand forward must be coordinated well with bending leg and loosening waist.

5. Play "Pipa"

"Pipa" is a traditional Chinese plucked string instrument. It looks a little like a guitar. In practicing this posture, you are asked to assume a position as if you were playing a "pipa."

Movements (continued from fig. 37): Bring your right foot close to the heel of your left foot, shift your weight onto your right foot, and lift your left foot and take a slight step forward to form a left empty step with heel touching the ground, knee slightly bent. In company with the movements of your legs, your left hand goes up from your left side to nose height with the arm slightly bent, palm facing right, and your right hand comes to the inside of your left elbow, palm facing left, thus both your hands and arms form a position as if playing a "pipa." Eyes now look at the forefinger of left hand (see figs. 38, 39, 40).

Fig. 38   Fig. 39   Fig. 40

Notes:

A. Keep your upper body upright and steady.

B. Do not protrude your buttocks.

C. Droop your shoulders, hang your elbows and relax your chest.

D. Do not raise your left hand directly to the front, but let it move in a curve upward from the left and then forward.

6. Step Back to Drive the Monkey Away (Left and Right)

Movement 1 (continued from fig. 40): Turn both your palms up and bring your right hand downward and backward, in a curve, past your right thigh and up to shoulder-height, palm still up. At the same time, move your left foot back with only the toes touching the ground. Eyes now look at left hand (see figs. 41, 42).

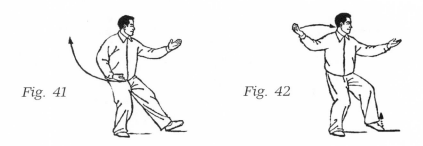

Fig. 41   Fig. 42

Movement 2: Bend your right elbow and push your right hand forward past your right ear to the front with palm facing outward. As your right hand moves forward, bring your left hand downward and backward in a curve past your left thigh, up to shoulder-height, palm up. At the same time, take a step back with your left foot, shift your weight backward onto it; turn your right palm up and let your eyes look at it (see figs. 43, 44, 45).

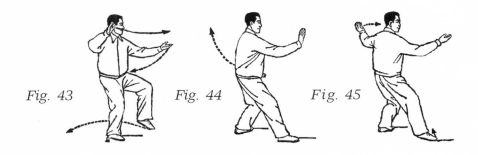

Fig. 43   Fig. 44   Fig. 45

Movement 3: Bend your left elbow and push your left hand forward past your left ear to the front with palm facing outward. As your left hand moves forward, bring your right hand downward and backward in a curve past your right thigh and up to your shoulder-height, palm up. At the same time, take a step back with your right foot, shift your weight backward onto it; turn your left palm up and let your eyes look at it (see figs. 46, 47, 48).

Fig. 46   Fig. 47   Fig. 48

Movement 4: Repeat Movement 2 (see figs. 49, 50, 51).

Fig. 49   Fig. 50

Fig. 51

Movement 5: Repeat Movement 3 (see figs. 52, 53, 54).

Fig. 52

Fig. 53

Fig. 54

Notes:

A. Do not straighten your arm when you push your hand forward; do not draw your front hand straight backward, but in a curve.

B. When you step back, let the toes of your back foot touch the ground first; at the same time, turn your front foot on the toes.

C. When you step back with your left foot, the left foot should be moved backward slightly to the left, and when you step back with your right foot, the right foot should be moved backward slightly to the right, only thus can you maintain good balance and make your steps steady.

D. When you step back, your eyes should first look in the direction of your body's turn and then at your front hand.

7. Grasp the Bird's Tail on the Left

The posture Grasp the Bird's Tail is composed of four basic movements. They are traditionally called "Peng" (meaning Ward Off, as shown in figs. 57, 58), "Lu" (meaning Roll Back, as shown in figs. 59, 60), "Ji" (meaning Press, as shown in figs. 61, 62) and "An" (meaning Push, as shown in fig. 66).

Movement 1 (continued from fig. 54): Turn your upper body slightly to the right, bring your left hand across your abdomen in a curve to lie below your right rib, palm up, and withdraw your right hand to rest in front of your chest, palm down; both hands now form a holding-ball position. At the same time, bring your left foot close to the right with toes touching the ground. Eyes now look at the right hand (see figs. 55, 56).

Fig. 55   Fig. 56

Movement 2: Take a step forward to the left with your left foot, and shift your weight onto it to form a left bow-shaped step. As you do so, move your left arm forward and upward to the left with hand at shoulder level, palm inward, and elbow slightly bent like a bow as if warding off a coming attack. At the same time, lower your right hand to the side of your right hip, palm downward. Eyes now look at the left forearm. This is called a Ward Off movement (see figs. 57, 58).

Fig. 57

Fig. 58

Note: During the Ward Off movement, keep both your shoulders sunk, your arms arced, and make sure that the separation of hands, relaxation of waist and bending of leg must be well coordinated.

Movement 3: Reach your left hand forward, palm down, and bring your right hand across your abdomen close to the wrist of your left hand, palm up; then let both your hands move backward, downward and upward to the right in a curve, until your right hand is level with your shoulder, palm upward, and your left hand is in front of your chest, palm inward. Meanwhile, slowly shift your weight onto the right leg. Eyes now look at right hand. This is called a Roll Back movement (see figs. 59, 60).

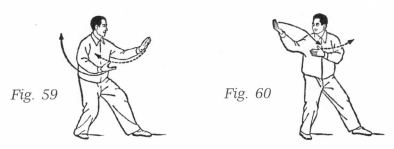

Fig. 59

Fig. 60

Note: When you do the Roll Back movement, do not bend your upper body forward or protrude your buttocks; move your roll-back arms along with the turning of your upper body; keep your left foot flat on the ground.

Movement 4: Bring your right hand back to the inside of the wrist of your left hand, then let both your hands press forward, the left palm inward and the right outward. At the same time, slowly shift your weight onto the left leg, forming a left bow-shaped step. Eyes now look at the wrist of the left hand. This is called a Press movement (see figs. 61, 62).

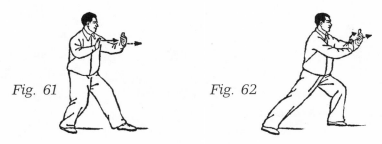

Fig. 61   Fig. 62

Note: When you Press forward with both hands, keep your upper body erect, your waist and hips relaxed. The pressing movement should be in harmony with loosening your waist and bowing your leg.

Movement 5: Separate your hands at about shoulder-width with both palms facing down, move your upper body back and shift your weight onto the right leg, holding up the toes of the left foot. At the same time, bring both your hands back to the sides of your chest, palms diagonally down. Eyes now look forward (see figs. 63, 64, 65).

Fig. 63   Fig. 64   Fig. 65

Movement 6: Push both hands forward and upward in a curve, with palms facing outward and level with shoulders. While doing so, shift your weight onto the left leg, forming a left bow-shaped step. Eyes now still look forward. This is called a Push movement (see figs. 65, 66).

Fig. 66

Note: When you push your hands forward, your upper body should be upright, your waist and hips relaxed. The pushing movement should be coordinated with loosening your waist and bending your leg. Both hands should move in a curve, both arms should be kept in an arc.

8. Grasp the Bird's Tail on the Right

Movement 1 (continued from fig. 66): Draw your upper body back, shift your weight onto the right leg, then turn your body to the right and move your left toes slightly inward. While doing so, let your right hand travel in a curve to the right side of your body, then go downward and across the abdomen to the left to finally rest below your left rib, palm up; bring your left hand back to lie in front of your chest, palm down, to form the holding-ball position with the right hand. At the same time, shift your weight back onto the left leg, bring your right foot close to the left, toes on the ground. Eyes now look at left hand (see figs. 67–70).

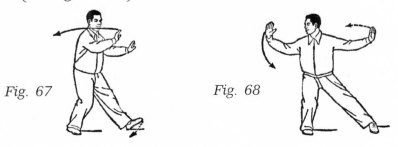

Fig. 67   Fig. 68

Fig. 69

Fig. 70

Movement 2: Practice according to the explanation of Movement 2 of Posture 7, but with opposite hands and feet (see figs. 71, 72).

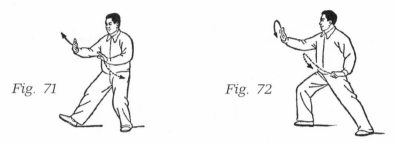

Fig. 71

Fig. 72

Movement 3: Practice according to the explanation of Movement 3 of Posture 7, but with opposite hands and feet (see figs. 73, 74).

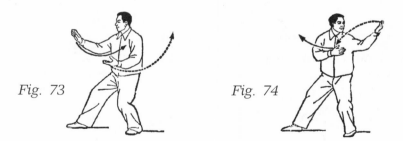

Fig. 73

Fig. 74

Movement 4: Practice according to the explanation of Movement 4, Posture 7, but with opposite hands and feet (see figs. 75, 76).

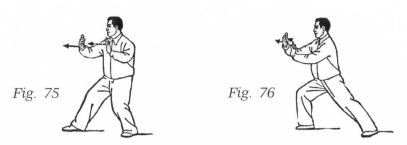

Fig. 75   Fig. 76

Movement 5: Practice according to the explanation of Movement 5, Posture 7, but with opposite hands and feet (see figs. 77, 78, 79).

Fig. 77   Fig. 78   Fig 79

Movement 6: Practice according to the explanation of Movement 6, Posture 7, but with opposite hands and feet (see fig. 80).

Fig. 80

Notes are the same as mentioned in Posture 7.

9. Single Whip

Movement 1 (continued from fig. 80): Draw back your upper body, shift your weight onto the left leg and turn your right toes in. As you do so, turn your upper body left, move your hands (the left higher than the right) across your chest to the left until your left arm is held horizontally on the left side of your body, and your right arm (bent at the elbow) rests in front of your chest. Eyes now look at left hand (see figs. 81, 82).

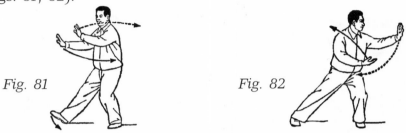

Fig. 81

Fig. 82

Movement 2: Slowly shift your weight onto the right leg, bring your left foot close to the right with toes touching the ground. At the same time, let your right hand move upward to the upper right side of your body, and bend your wrist to form a beaked hand (fingers and thumb together); let your left hand move downward, across your abdomen to the right and then upward to rest in front of your right shoulder, palm inward. Eyes now look at left hand (see figs. 83, 84).

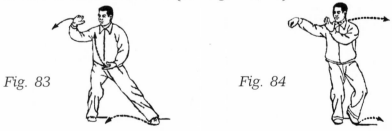

Fig. 83

Fig. 84

Movement 3: Turn your upper body slightly left, take a step to the left with your left foot and shift your weight onto it, forming a left bow-shaped step. At the same time, turn your left palm outward and push it out to the left with fingers being level with your eyes. Let your arms bend slightly to keep your shoulders sinking and elbows drooping. Eyes now look at left hand (see figs. 85, 86).

Fig. 85   *Fig. 86*

Notes:

A. During the sequence of various movements, pay attention to keeping your upper body erect, waist relaxed, and shoulders hung down.

B. Pushing your left palm out to the left should be synchronized with turning your upper body left and forming the left bow-shaped step with your left foot; all the interim movements should also be done in harmony.

C. At the end of the posture, let your right elbow slightly hang down and your left elbow be in line with your left knee.

10. Wave Hands like Clouds

Movement 1 (continued from fig. 86): Shift your weight onto the right foot, turn your left toes inward, and slowly turn your upper body to the right. In the meantime, let your left hand move across your abdomen and up to rest in front of your right shoulder, palm inclined inward; let your right hand change from the beaked hand into an open palm (facing outward). Eyes now look at left hand (see figs. 87, 88, 89).

Fig. 87   *Fig. 88*   *Fig. 89*

Movement 2: Shift your weight slowly onto the left foot, move your left hand across your face to the left side with palm turning gradually to the left, and bring your right hand down, across your abdomen and up to rest in front of your left shoulder, palm inclined inward. At the same time, draw your right foot near the left, and keep them parallel to each other and 4–5 inches apart. Eyes now look at right hand (see figs. 90, 91).

Fig. 90   *Fig. 91*

Movement 3: Shift your weight onto the right foot, move your right hand across your face in a curve to the right side with palm turning gradually to the right; bring your left hand down, in a curve, across your abdomen and up to rest in front of your right shoulder, palm inclined inward. At the same time, turn your right palm to the right and take a step to the left with the left foot. Eyes now look at left hand (see figs. 92, 93, 94).

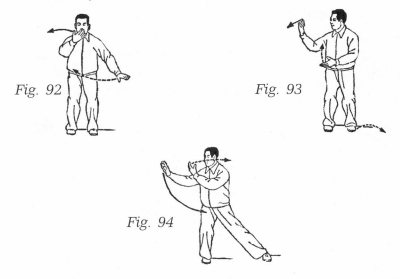

Fig. 92   *Fig. 93*

Fig. 94

Movement 4: Repeat Movement 2 (see figs. 95, 96).

Fig. 95   Fig. 96

Movement 5: Repeat Movement 3 (see figs. 97, 98, 99).

Fig. 97   Fig. 98

Fig. 99

Movement: 6: Repeat Movement 2 (see figs. 100, 101).

Fig. 100   Fig. 101

Notes:

A. Take your lumbar spine as the axis when turning your body, move your arms along with the turn in your waist, and let your eyes follow the hand in crossing your face.

B. As you take sidesteps, move your legs slowly and steadily, pay attention to keeping your balance and avoiding up-and-down actions.

C. Keep your waist and hips relaxed, and do not pull your shoulders up when moving your arms.

D. The movements of your arms should be natural and round, and at an even speed.

11. Single Whip

Movement 1 (continued from fig. 101): Move your right hand in a curve to the upper right side and let it change into a beaked hand; bring your left hand down, across your abdomen and up to lie in front of your right shoulder, palm inward. While doing so, shift your weight onto the right foot, and draw your left foot near the right, toes on the ground. Eyes now look at left hand (see figs. 102, 103, 104).

Fig. 102

Fig. 103

Fig. 104

Movement 2: Turn your upper body slightly left, take a step forward with the left foot, and shift your weight onto it, forming a left bow-shaped step. While doing so, turn your left palm outward and push it out to the left with fingers being level with your eyes. Let both your arms bend slightly to keep your shoulders sinking and elbows drooping. Eyes now look at left hand (see figs. 105, 106).

Fig. 105   *Fig. 106*

Notes are the same as mentioned in Posture 9.

12. Stroke the Horse from Above

Movement 1 (continued from fig. 106): Draw your right foot closer to the left while changing your right beaked hand into an open palm and turn both palms to face upward with elbows bending slightly. At the same time, turn your body slightly to the right, shift your weight back onto the right leg, and lift your left heel to form a left empty step. Eyes now look at left hand (see fig. 107).

Fig. 107

Movement 2: Push your right hand forward by the side of your right ear, palm facing forward, fingers at eyebrow level; bring your left hand back to the left side of your waist, palm facing upward. Eyes now look at right hand (see fig. 108).

Fig. 108

Notes:

A. When you shift your weight onto the right foot and form an empty step with your left foot, keep your upper body upright and do not protrude your buttocks.

B. Push your right hand forward in a curve, with elbow slightly bent and fingers pointing up.

13. *Kick with Right Heel*

In practicing this posture, you are asked to strike with your heel rather than toes. Thus, it is a little different from what is usually called a "kick."

Movement 1 (continued from fig. 108): Move your left hand (palm up) upward in front of your chest, passing over your right wrist; separate your hands and bring them down and round in a curve from both sides of your body with palms diagonally downward. In the meantime, take a step forward with your left foot and shift your weight onto it to form a left bow-shaped step (see figs. 109, 110, 111).

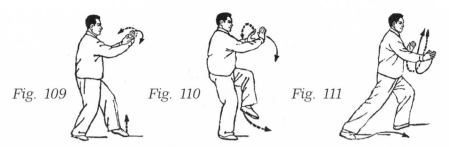

Fig. 109   Fig. 110   Fig. 111

Movement 2: Bring both your hands back in a curve to cross in front of your chest, palms in, the right hand outside the left. At the same time, draw your right foot close to the left, toes on the ground. Eyes now look at the space between your hands (see fig. 112).

Fig. 112

Movement 3: Separate your hands and hold them horizontally on both sides of your body with wrists being level with shoulders and palms facing outward. At the same time, lift your right foot and gently kick out, heel first with toes drawing back. Your right leg and right arm come into an overlapping position, leg below the arm. Eyes now look at right hand (see figs. 113, 114).

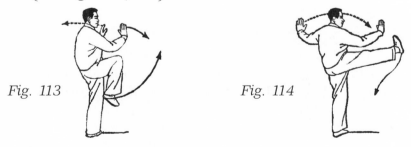

Fig. 113   Fig. 114

Notes:

A. Do not let your upper body lean either forward or backward so as to assure good balance.

B. Separating your hands should be synchronized with extending your right foot forward.

C. Your left leg should be slightly bent as your right foot kicks out.

D. At the end of the posture, your right arm should be vertically parallel to your right leg.

14. Hit the Opponent's Ears with Both Fists

Movement 1 (continued from fig. 114): Bend your right leg at the knee, keep the thigh parallel to the ground and the toes pointing downward. Bring your left hand close to the right. Then let both hands drop in a curve by both sides of your right knee, palms up. Eyes look forward (see figs. 115, 116).

Fig. 115

Fig. 116

Movement 2: Alight your right foot, and shift your weight forward onto it, making a right bow-shaped step. At the same time, turn your hands into fists, and let them separate to both sides, moving forward and round in a circle to form a pincerlike shape in front of you, at eye level, with fist holes (formed by the thumb and index fingers of each hand) facing obliquely downward. The distance between fists should be about 6 inches. Eyes now look at right fist (see figs. 117, 118).

Fig. 117

Fig. 118

Notes:

A. Hold your head and neck upright, relax your chest and waist and keep your shoulders sunk and elbows drooped during the whole process.

B. Your fists should not be made tightly, but rather loosely.

C. At the conclusion of the posture, both your arms should be maintained in an arc-shape.

5. *Turn Round and Kick with Left Heel*

Movement 1 (continued from fig. 118): Bend your left knee, slowly shift your weight onto the left leg, and turn your body left and your right toes inward. While doing so, open your fists into palms, and move them apart in a slight curve to both sides. Both your palms should face outward. Eyes now look at left hand (see figs. 119, 120).

Fig. 119

Fig. 120

Movement 2: Shift your weight back onto the right leg, draw your left foot close to the right, toes on the ground. At the same time, move your hands down, then inward and up in an arc to cross in front of your chest, both palms inward, the left outside the right. Eyes now look at the space between the two hands (see figs. 121, 122).

Fig. 121

Fig. 122

Movement 3: Separate your arms and hold them horizontally on both sides of your body with wrists being level with shoulders and palms facing outward. At the same time, lift your left foot and gently kick out, heel first with toes drawing back. Your left leg and left arm come into an overlapping position, leg below the arm. Eyes now look at left hand (see figs. 123, 124).

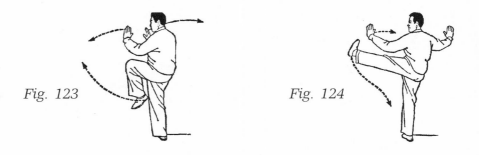

Fig. 123

Fig. 124

Notes are the same as mentioned in Posture 13, only the direction, hand and foot referred to are opposite.

16. Squat Down and Stand on Left Leg

In practicing this posture, you will end your movements in a position such as a Golden Cock stands on one leg—the left leg.

Movement 1 (continued from fig. 124): Bend your left knee and draw your left foot back to keep the left thigh in a horizontal position. Turn your right palm into a beaked hand, and move your left palm to the right in a curve to lie in front of your right armpit. Eyes now look at left hand (see figs. 125, 126).

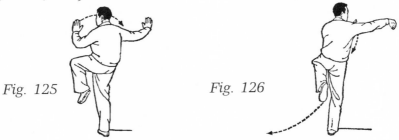

Fig. 125　　　　　　　　*Fig. 126*

Movement 2: Slowly squat down as far as your right knee can bend, and extend your left leg to the left side to form a stretched step. As you do so, let your left hand descend to your left thigh and then slide forward along the inside of your left leg, palm outward. Eyes now look at left hand (see figs. 127, 128).

Fig. 127　　　　　　　　*Fig. 128*

Notes:

A. When squatting down on your right leg, do not let your upper body lean too far forward.

B. In forming the stretched step with your left leg, try to straighten the leg as far as you can and keep the toes of the left foot slightly inward and the sole fully touching the ground.

Movement 3: Turn your left toes outward, slowly straighten your right leg with toes turning inward and shift your weight forward onto the left foot to form a left bow-shaped step. Meanwhile, move your left hand forward and up to shoulder level with palm facing out. Eyes now look at left hand (see fig. 129).

Fig. 129

Movement 4: Slowly lift your right leg with knee fully bent and toes pointing downward, forming a position of standing on one leg—the left leg. At the same time, your right beaked hand turns into an open palm and moves forward and upward with your right leg to shoulder level, elbow above the knee, palm facing left; your left hand descends to your left hip, palm down. Eyes now look at right hand (see figs. 130, 131).

Fig. 130

Fig. 131

Notes:

A. Bend your left leg slightly.

B. Keep your upper body upright and steady.

17. Squat Down and Stand on Right Leg

In practicing this posture, you will end your movements in a position such as a Golden Cock stands on one leg—the right leg.

Movement 1 (continued from fig. 131): Bring your right foot down in front of the left with toes touching the ground; then, pivoting on your left toes, turn your body left. At the same time, your left hand stretches backward horizontally and turns into a beaked hand; your right hand moves left in a curve to rest in front of your left armpit. Eyes now look at right hand (see figs. 132, 133).

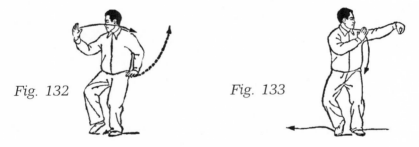

Fig. 132   Fig. 133

Movement 2: Practice according to the explanation of Movement 2, Posture 16, but from the opposite side and with opposite hands and feet (see figs. 134, 135).

Fig. 134   Fig. 135

Movement 3: Practice according to the explanation of Movement 3, Posture 16, but from the opposite side and with opposite hands and feet (see fig. 136).

Fig. 136

Movement 4: Practice according to the explanation of Movement 4, Posture 16, but from the opposite side and with opposite hands and feet (see figs. 137, 138).

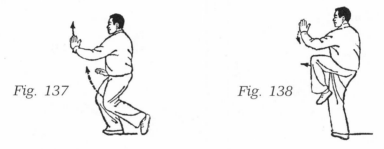

Fig. 137   *Fig. 138*

Notes are the same as mentioned in Posture 16, only the hand, foot or leg referred to are opposite.

18. *Fair Lady Works with Shuttles (Left and Right)*

In practicing this posture, you are asked to assume the positions of a fair lady working with shuttles back and forth on the loom.

Movement 1 (continued from fig. 138): Turn your body a little to the left, let your left foot alight on the ground with toes pointing outward, lift your right heel off the ground and shift your weight onto the left foot. As you do so, bring both your hands into a holding-ball position in front of your left chest, the left hand on top. Then draw your right foot close to the inside of the left, with toes touching the ground. Eyes now look at the left forearm (see figs. 139, 140, 141).

Fig. 139   Fig. 140   Fig. 141

Movement 2: Take a step to the right with your right foot, and slowly shift your weight onto it, forming a right bow-shaped step. At the same time, your right hand goes up past your face to lie in front of your forehead (as if protecting it) with palm facing diagonally upward, and your left hand pushes out across your body, at nose level, palm outward. Eyes now look at left hand (see figs. 142, 143, 144).

Fig. 142   Fig. 143

Fig. 144

Movement 3: Slightly shift your weight back onto the left leg. Turn your right toes a little outward, and shift your weight forward onto the right leg again. Then draw your left foot close to the inside of the right foot with toes touching the ground. At the same time, bring both hands into a holding-ball position in front of your right chest, the right hand on top. Eyes now look at the right forearm (see figs. 145, 146).

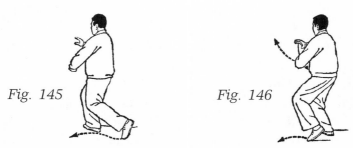

Fig. 145   Fig. 146

Movement 4: Repeat Movement 2, but in the opposite direction and with opposite hands and feet, as figs. 147, 148, 149 show:

Fig. 147   Fig. 148   Fig. 149

Notes:

A. Avoid pulling your shoulder up when raising your hand to the forehead.

B. Do not lean forward with your upper body while pushing your hand forward.

C. Coordinate pushing hand forward with bending your front leg and moving your upper body forward. (These are applicable to either side.)

19. Needle at Sea Bottom

To complete this posture you are asked to act as if fishing for a needle from the bottom of the sea.

Movements (continued from fig. 149): Take a small step forward with the right foot, keeping it close to the heel of the left; then shift your weight back onto the right leg which is now slightly bent at the knee, and let your left foot move a little forward with toes alighting on the ground, forming a left empty step. In company with these movements, bring your right hand to the side of your right ear, then let it drop in front of your body with fingers pointing downward; your left hand descends to the side of your left hip. Eyes now look slantingly downward (see figs. 150, 151).

Fig. 150   *Fig. 151*

Notes:

A. Avoid bowing your head, protruding your buttocks or pulling your shoulder down while your right hand is dropping.

B. Your weight is on your right leg, and your left leg should be moderately bent at the knee.

C. At the end of the posture, your upper body should not lean too far forward.

20. Fend Off and Push Away with Arms

Movements (continued from fig. 151): Turn your upper body slightly to the right, take a small step forward with the left leg, and shift your weight forward onto it to form a left bow-shaped step. At the same time, your right hand rises in front of your body in a curve to lie above your forehead with palm facing obliquely outward, so that your right arm comes into a semicircle; your left hand pushes out horizontally with palm facing forward and being level with the tip of your nose. Eyes now look at left hand (see figs. 152, 153, 154).

Fig. 152

Fig. 153

Fig. 154

Notes:

A. Keep your upper body erect in a natural state with waist and hips relaxed.

B. Do not straighten your left arm when you push it out.

C. Keep both your shoulders drooped and your back muscles fully stretched.

D. Synchronize your weight shift with the movements of your arms and legs.

21. *Turn, Intercept, and Punch*

Movement 1 (continued from fig. 154): Slowly bend your right leg to shift your weight back onto it and turn your left toes inward; turn your body 180 degrees to the right, then shift your weight again onto the left leg. At the same time, with the turning of your body, move your right palm to the right, down (turning into a fist now) and across your abdomen in a curve to lie by the left side of your waist, the back of the fist upward; raise your left palm up in a curve to rest above your forehead, facing diagonally upward. Eyes now look ahead (see figs. 155, 156).

Fig. 155   *Fig. 156*

Movement 2: Turn your body right, throw out your right fist across your chest, the back of the fist downward, and let your left palm fall to the side of your left hip. Meanwhile, draw back your right foot and then step forward with it again, with toes pointing outward. Eyes now look at the right fist (see figs. 157, 158).

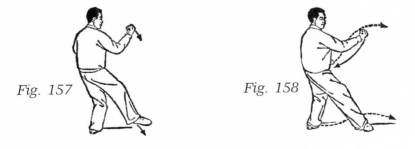

Fig. 157   *Fig. 158*

Movement 3: Shift your weight forward onto the right leg and take a step forward with the left leg. At the same time, move your left hand a little to the left, then up and forward in a curve to assume an intercept position, palm diagonally downward; draw your right fist back to the right side of your waist, the back of the fist downward. Eyes now look at left hand (see figs. 159, 160).

Fig. 159   *Fig. 160*

Movement 4: Shift your weight forward onto the left leg, assuming a left bow-shaped step. At the same time, punch forward with your right fist at chest level, with fist hole facing upward, and let your left hand attach to the inner side of the right forearm. Eyes now look at the right fist (see fig. 161).

Fig. 161

Notes:

A. When you strike out with your right fist, do not straighten your right arm, but let your right shoulder go slightly forward.

B. Keep your shoulders and elbows relaxed, and do not clench your fist tightly.

22. As if Blocking and Closing

Movement 1 (continued from fig. 161): Stretch out your left hand from below the right wrist, palm up, turn your right fist into a palm, also facing upward, and then slowly withdraw both palms in a curve toward the sides of your chest. At the same time, bend your right leg, draw back your upper body, hold up your left toes and shift your weight back onto the right leg. Eyes now look forward (see figs. 162, 163, 164).

Fig. 162   *Fig. 163*   *Fig. 164*

Movement 2: When you draw both palms nearer your chest, turn them down and lower them to your abdomen, then push them forward and up again until your wrists are level with your shoulders. Both palms should face forward. At the same time, shift your weight forward onto the left leg, forming a left bow-shaped step. Eyes now look at the space between two palms (see figs. 165, 166, 167).

Fig. 165   *Fig. 166*   *Fig. 167*

Notes:

A. As shifting your weight back, avoid leaning your upper body backward or sticking your buttocks out.

B. Bend your elbows gently and keep them a little away from your body when you draw your hands backward.

C. Never move your hands in a straight line during pulling them forward.

D. The action of shifting your weight to the right foot should synchronize with that of drawing your hands to your chest.

E. At the end of the posture, your extended hands should be about shoulder-width apart.

23. Cross Hands

This posture should be finished with both hands coming into a criss-cross shape in front of your chest.

Movement 1 (continued from fig. 167): Shift your weight back onto your right foot and turn your body to the right. Along with the turning of your body, move your left toes inward and right toes outward, and change your legs into a right bow-shaped step. At the same time, separate your hands outward to the sides of your body with elbows drooping slightly and palms facing diagonally downward. Eyes now look at right hand (see figs. 168, 169).

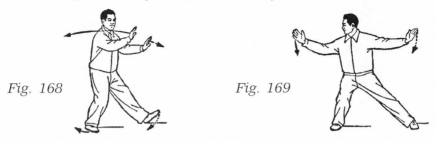

Fig. 168   *Fig. 169*

Movement 2: Slowly shift your weight onto the left leg, turn your right toes inward and draw back your right foot, keeping it shoulder-width apart from the left, then gradually straighten both legs with toes pointing forward. In the meantime, both hands descend past your abdomen in arc-like fashion, then travel inward and upward to cross each other in front of your chest, palms in, right hand on the outside. Eyes now look horizontally forward (see figs. 170, 171).

Fig. 170   *Fig. 171*

Notes:

A. As your hands come into a crisscross, both your arms should be kept in an arc-shape, with elbows slightly bent and shoulders hanging down.

B. When you straighten your legs, keep your body erect, hold your chin slightly in, and avoid tensing any part of your body.

24. Concluding Posture

Movements (continued from fig. 171): Turn both your hands outward, let them separate and descend slowly to the outsides of your thighs with your palms facing inward and your fingers pointing downward. Eyes now look horizontally forward (see figs. 172, 173, 174).

Fig. 172   *Fig. 173*   *Fig. 174*

Notes:

A. In lowering your hands to the outsides of your thighs, you should keep your palms facing downward and your fingertips pointing forward as if your were pressing something down.

B. When your hands move down, exhale slowly and relax your whole body.

C. You may conclude your practice with some supplementary exercises or a little walk.

Diagram Showing the Movements and Positions of the Feet from the First Posture to the Last One of the Simplified T'ai Chi Ch'uan

The footprints made of dotted line represent the left foot; the footprints made of solid line represent the right foot. The numerals without brackets indicate the order of postures; the numerals in brackets indicate the repetition of a movement or the left and right styles of the same stance. Those footprints without numerals indicate the change from one posture to another.

Indicates that the ball of the foot is touching the ground.

Indicates that the heel of the foot is touching the ground.

Indicates that in performing "Stand on One Leg" one foot is lifted off the ground with the knee fully bent.

Indicates that one foot is extended in the air with the leg stretched while performing "Kick with Heel."

Indicates the position where the tip of the foot is set on the ground during changes.

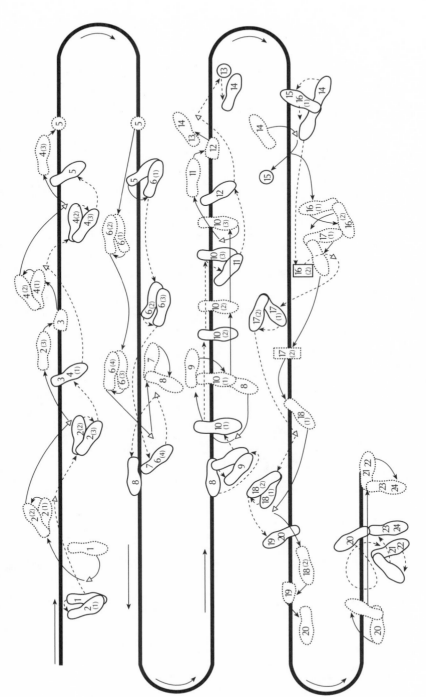

Simplified T'ai Chi Ch'uan.

CHAPTER V

Standard T'ai Chi Ch'uan

The Standard T'ai Chi Ch'uan consists of 88 postures and is generally divided into three series. The first series covers 13 postures, the second series, 34 postures, and the third series, 41 postures. You may practice the complete form or choose one series or two series to do according to your physical strength and the given time. All of the 88 postures and their component movements are illustrated by detailed, step-by-step explanations and figures as follows.

1. Preparation Posture

Movement 1: Stand erect with both hands at your sides. Your heels should be slightly touching. Actually you are expected to adopt the position of "standing at attention" in order to concentrate your mind, remove distracting thoughts, and prepare for the practice (see fig. 1).

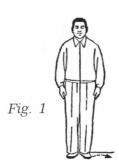

Fig. 1

Movement 2: Separate your feet by moving the left foot to the left. They are requested to be parallel to each other about shoulder-width apart. Your weight should be evenly distributed between them. Your shoulders should be naturally sunk, your lower jaw slightly drawn back, your chest muscle slackened, your back straight but a bit round. Furthermore, you should try to iron out any tensions you produced at the beginning. Eyes now look horizontally forward (see fig. 2).

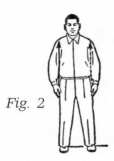

Fig. 2

2. Starting Posture

Movement 1 (continued from fig. 2): Gently raise your arms in front of you, palms facing downward, until your hands reach shoulder-height (see fig. 3).

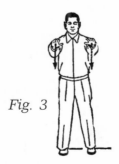

Fig. 3

Movement 2: Keep your upper body upright. Bend your knees slightly and squat down gently. As you do so, slowly lower your arms with shoulders sinking, elbows drooping and vertically opposite your knees. Eyes now look straight ahead (see fig. 4).

Fig. 4

Notes:

A. Do not allow your buttocks to protrude while your body is squatting down.

B. The descending of your arms and the squatting of your body must be well coordinated.

C. In this posture your weight is also distributed evenly on both legs.

3. *Grasp the Bird's Tail*

This posture will be repeated many times during performance. It includes four movements, which are traditionally called "Ward Off" (see figs. 7, 8), "Roll Back" (see figs. 9, 10, 11), "Press" (see figs. 12, 13) and "Push" (see figs. 16, 17). Now, let us illustrate in detail.

Movement 1 (continued from fig. 4): Turn your body slightly right and move the toes of your right foot slightly outward. With the turning of the body, your left hand travels to the right in a curve to lie below the right rib, palm up, and your right hand goes up and back in a curve to rest in front of your chest, palm down, both hands now forming a holding-ball position. Meanwhile, draw your left foot close to the inside of the right foot, toes on the ground. Eyes now look at right hand (see fig. 5).

Fig. 5

Movement 2: Take a step forward to the left with your left foot, and shift your weight onto it to form a left "bow-shaped step" (it is usually called "forward lunge" in terms of martial arts). As you do so, move your left arm forward and upward to the left with hand at shoulder-level, palm inward, and elbow slightly bent like a bow as if warding off a coming attack. At the same time, lower your right hand to the side of your right hip, palm downward. Eyes now look at left forearm (see fig. 6).

Fig. 6

Movement 3: Turn your body slightly to the left, bring your left hand back in front of your chest, palm down, and let your right hand travel to the left and across your abdomen in a curve to lie below your left rib, palm up, to form a holding-ball position with the left hand. Meanwhile, draw your right foot close to the inside of the left foot, toes on the ground. Now your weight is on the left leg, and your eyes look at the left hand (see fig. 7).

Fig. 7

Movement 4: Take a step to the right with your right foot and shift your weight onto it to form a right bow-shaped step. Meanwhile, your right arm stretches to the right and upward to shoulder-level, palm inward, as if warding off an attack, and your left hand descends to the side of your left hip, palm downward. Eyes now look at right forearm. This is called a Ward Off movement (see fig. 8).

Fig. 8

Note: When you do the Ward Off movement (left or right), you are asked to droop both shoulders, keep both arms in an arc-shape, and synchronize the separation of hands with relaxation of waist and bending of leg.

Movement 5: Reach your right hand forward, palm down, and bring your left hand across your abdomen and upward close to the wrist of your right hand, palm up. Then draw both hands backward, downward and upward to the left in a curve, until the left hand is level with your shoulder, palm upward, and the right hand is in front of your chest, palm inward. At the same time, slowly shift your weight onto the left leg. Eyes now look at left hand. This is called a Roll Back movement (see figs. 9, 10, 11).

Fig. 9

Fig. 10

Fig. 11

Note: When you do the Roll Back movement, do not bend your upper body forward or protrude your buttocks; move your rolling back arms to the left along with the turning of your upper body; keep your right foot flat on the ground.

Movement 6: Bring your left hand back to the inside of the wrist of your right hand, then let both hands press forward, the right palm inward and the left outward. Meanwhile, slowly shift your weight onto the right leg, forming a right bow-shaped step. Eyes now look at the wrist of right hand. This is called a Press movement (see figs. 12, 13).

Fig. 12

Fig. 13

Note: When you press forward with your hands, keep your upper body erect, your waist and your hips relaxed. The pressing movement should be in harmony with loosening your waist and bowing your leg.

Movement 7: Separate your hands at about shoulder-width with both palms facing down, move your upper body back and shift your weight onto the left leg, holding up the toes of the right foot. At the same time, bring both your hands back to the sides of your chest, palms diagonally downward. Eyes now look horizontally forward (see figs. 14, 15, 16).

Fig. 14

Fig. 15

Fig. 16

Movement 8: Push both hands forward and upward with palms facing outward and wrists being level with your shoulders. While doing this, shift your weight onto the right leg to assume a right bow-shaped step. Eyes still look horizontally forward. This is called a Push movement (see fig. 17).

Fig. 17

Note: When you Push your hands forward, your upper body should be upright, your waist and hips relaxed. The pushing movement should be in harmony with loosening your waist and bowing your leg. Both your hands should move in a curve; both your arms should be kept in an arc-shape.

4. Single Whip

Movement 1 (continued from fig. 17): Gently draw back your upper body, shift your weight onto the left leg and turn your right toes in. At the same time, turn your upper body left, move both hands (the left higher than the right) across your chest to the left until your left arm is held horizontally on the left side of your body, and your right arm (bent at the elbow) lies in front of your chest. Eyes now look at left hand (see figs. 18, 19).

Fig. 18

Fig. 19

Movement 2: Slowly shift your weight onto the right leg, bring your left foot close to the right with toes touching the ground. Meanwhile, let your right hand move upward to the upper right side of your body, and bend your wrist to form a beaked hand (fingers and thumb together); let your left hand move downward, across your abdomen and then upward to rest in front of your shoulder, palm inward. Eyes now look at left hand (see figs. 20, 21).

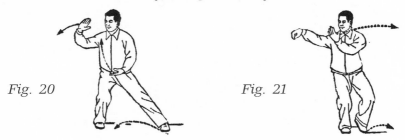

Fig. 20   *Fig. 21*

Movement 3: Turn your upper body slightly left, take a step forward to the left with your left foot and shift your weight onto it to form a left bow-shaped step. At the same time, turn your left palm outward and push it out to the left with fingers being level with your eyes. Let both your arms bend slightly so as to keep your shoulders sinking and elbows drooping. Eyes now look at left hand (see fig. 22).

Fig. 22

Notes:

A. During the sequence of various movements, pay attention to keeping your upper body erect, waist relaxed, and shoulders sunk.

B. Pushing your left palm out to the left should be synchronized with turning your upper body left and forming the left bow-shaped step with your left foot, and all the interim movements should also be done in harmony.

C. At the conclusion, let your right elbow slightly hang down and your left elbow be in line with your left knee.

5. *Lifting Hands*

Movements (continued from fig. 22): Slowly draw back your upper body, bend your right leg and shift your weight onto it; turn your body right and your left toes in, then shift your weight onto the left leg again. At the same time, turn your right beaked hand into an open palm, and move it to the left to stop in front of your face with palm facing left, fingers pointing up and being level with your eyebrow; bring your left hand near the inside of your right arm with palm facing right and being about chest-height. Meanwhile, lift your right foot and let it alight in front of the left, heel on the ground, assuming a right empty step. Eyes now look at the forefinger of right hand (see figs. 23, 24).

Fig. 23   Fig. 24

Notes:

A. As shifting your weight or turning your torso, keep your upper body steady and natural, and avoid protruding your buttocks.

B. When your right heel touches the ground, your right knee should bend slightly to form a right empty step.

C. At the end of the posture, both your arms should be slightly bent with shoulders drooped, elbows hung down, and chest muscles relaxed.

6. White Crane Spreads Its Wings

Movements (continued from fig. 24): Turn your body slightly to the left, bring both hands to the left side of your body and assume a holding-ball position with the left hand above the right. Meanwhile, move your right foot a little backward with toes turned in. Then, raise your right hand to the right side of your head (but not higher than the head), palm inward, and lower your left hand to the side of your left hip, palm downward. Simultaneously, shift your weight onto the right leg and move your left foot a little forward with toes touching the ground, forming a left empty step. Eyes now look forward (see figs. 25, 26, 27).

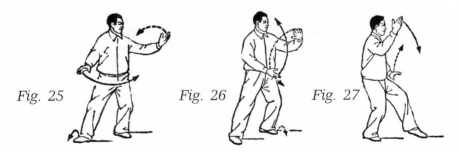

Fig. 25   Fig. 26   Fig. 27

Notes:

A. Do not throw out your chest and square your shoulders at the end of the posture.

B. Your left knee should slightly bend, and both your arms should be kept in an arc-shape.

7.   *Brush Left Knee and Twist Step*

Movement 1 (continued from fig. 27): Lower your right hand in front of your body toward your right knee, then let it go back and up, in a curve, to ear level, palm up; move your left hand right and up, in a curve, to the right side of your chest, palm down. At the same time, turn your upper body to the right. Eyes now look at right hand (see figs. 28, 29, 30).

Fig. 28   *Fig. 29*   *Fig. 30*

Movement 2: Turn your upper body left, take a step forward to the left with the left foot, and shift your weight onto it to make a left bow-shaped step. Meanwhile, bring your right hand back from behind and push it forward by the side of your right ear, keeping it at nose-level, palm outward; let your left hand fall down and brush past your left knee to rest beside your left hip. Eyes now look at the forefinger of right hand (see fig. 31).

Fig. 31

Notes:

A. While pushing your hand forward or moving it backward, keep your upper body erect, sink your shoulder, droop your elbow, and relax your waist and hips.

B. Synchronize pushing your hand forward with relaxing your waist and bowing your leg.

8. Play *"Pipa"*

"Pipa," a traditional Chinese plucked string instrument, looks similar to a guitar both in structure and form. In practicing this posture you are asked to end with a gesture as if playing a "pipa."

Movements (continued from fig. 31): Bring your right foot close to the heel of the left foot, raise your left foot and take a small step forward to form a left empty step, with heel touching the ground, knee slightly bent. Your weight is now on your right leg. In pace with the movements of your legs, your left hand rises in front of your body to nose-level with arm slightly bent, palm facing right, and right hand comes to the inside of your left elbow, palm facing left, thus both hands and arms form a position as if playing a "pipa." Eyes now look at the forefinger of left hand (see figs. 32, 33).

Fig. 32   *Fig. 33*

Notes:

A. Keep your body upright and steady, do not protrude your buttocks.

B. Sink your shoulders, droop your elbows, and relax your chest.

C. Do not raise your left hand directly to the front, but move it in a curve upward from the left and then forward.

9. Brush Knee and Twist Step (Left and Right)

Movement 1 (continued from fig. 33): Slowly lower your right hand, then let it go backward and upward in a curve to ear level, palm up, and bring your left hand downward and backward in a curve to the right side of your chest, palm down. Meanwhile, turn your upper body to the right and draw your left foot back with toes touching the ground. Eyes now look at right hand (see fig. 34).

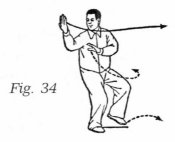

Fig. 34

Movement 2: Turn your upper body left, take a step forward to the left with the left foot, and shift your weight onto it to form a left bow-shaped step. Meanwhile, bring your right hand back from behind and push it forward by the side of your right ear, holding at nose-level, palm outward; let your left hand fall down and brush past your left knee to rest beside your left hip. Eyes now look at the forefinger of right hand (see fig. 35).

Fig. 35

Movement 3: Gently draw your upper body back and bend your right leg to shift your weight onto it. Turn your left toes slightly outward, and turn your body to the left at the same time. Then bend your left leg to assume a left bow-shaped step, and bring the right foot close to the left with toes touching the ground. As you do so, turn over your left hand and let it move backward and upward in a curve, to ear level, palm up; let your right hand, with the turning of your body, come back to rest in front of your left shoulder, palm down. Eyes now look at left hand (see figs. 36, 37, 38).

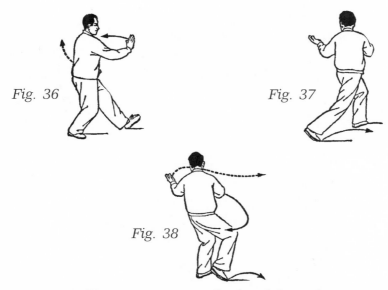

Fig. 36

Fig. 37

Fig. 38

Movement 4: Turn your upper body right, take a step forward to the right with the right foot, and shift your weight onto it to form a right bow-shaped step. Meanwhile, bring your left hand back from behind and push it forward by the side of your left ear, holding at nose-level, palm outward; let your right hand fall down and brush past your right knee to rest beside your right hip. Eyes now look at the forefinger of left hand (see fig. 39).

Fig. 39

Movement 5: Practice according to the explanation of Movement 3, but with opposite hands and feet (see figs. 40, 41).

Fig. 40   Fig. 41

Movement 6: Repeat Movement 2 (see figs. 42, 43).

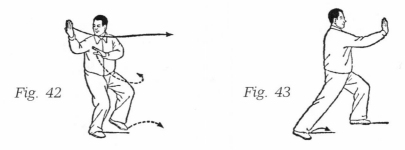

Fig. 42   Fig. 43

Notes are the same as mentioned in Posture 7.

10. Play "Pipa"

Both movements and notes are the same as mentioned in Posture 8 (see figs. 44, 45).

Fig. 44   Fig. 45

11. Step Forward, Intercept, and Punch

Movement 1 (continued from fig. 45): Turn your body left and your left toes outward. As you do so, turn your left palm to face downward, and change your right palm into a fist and let it go down and to the left in a curve, the back of the fist upward. At the same time, shift your weight onto the left leg and bend your right leg a little, heel lifted and turned out. Eyes now look at left hand (see fig. 46).

Fig. 46

Movement 2: Turn your body to the right, throw out your right fist across your chest in a curve, the back of the fist downward, and let your left palm fall to the side of your left hip. Meanwhile, your right foot takes a step forward with toes pointing outward. Eyes now look at right hand (see fig. 47).

Fig. 47

Movement 3: Shift your weight forward onto the right leg and take a step forward with the left foot. At the same time, move your left hand a little to the left, then up and forward in a curve to assume an intercepting position, palm obliquely downward, and draw your right fist back to the right side of your waist, the back of the fist downward. Eyes now look at left hand (see fig. 48).

Fig. 48

Movement 4: Shift your weight forward onto the left leg to assume a left bow-shaped step. Meanwhile, punch your right fist forward at chest level with fist hole (formed by the thumb and index finger) facing upward, and attach your left hand to the inside of your right forearm. Eyes now look at right fist (see fig. 49).

Fig. 49

Notes:

A. When you strike out with your right fist, do not straighten your right arm, but let your right shoulder move slightly forward.

B. Do not clench your fist tightly, keep your shoulders and elbows relaxed.

12. As if Blocking and Closing

Movement 1 (continued from fig. 49): Stretch out your left hand from below the wrist of your right hand, palm upward; turn your right fist into an open palm, also facing upward; then slowly withdraw both palms toward the sides of your chest. Meanwhile, bend your right leg, draw back your upper body, hold up your left toes and shift your weight onto the right leg. Eyes now look forward (see figs. 50, 51).

Fig. 50   Fig. 51

Movement 2: When you draw both palms nearer your chest, turn them down and lower them to your abdomen, then push them forward and up again until your wrists are level with your shoulders. Both palms should face forward. At the same time, shift your weight forward onto the left leg to form a left bow-shaped step. Eyes now look at the space between palms (see figs. 52, 53).

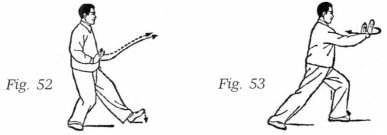

Fig. 52   Fig. 53

Notes:

A. While shifting your weight back, avoid leaning your upper body backward or sticking your buttock out.

B. Bend your elbows gently and keep them a little away from your body when you draw your hands backward.

C. Never move your hands in a straight line during pulling them backward or pushing them forward.

D. The action of shifting your weight to your right foot should synchronize with that of drawing your hands to your chest.

E. At the end of the posture, your extended hands should be about shoulder-width apart.

13. Cross Hands

Movement 1 (continued from fig. 53): Shift your weight back onto the right leg and turn your body right. Along with the turning of your body, move your left toes inward and right toes outward, and change your legs into a right bow-shaped step. At the same time, separate your hands outward to the sides of your body with elbows drooping slightly and palms facing diagonally downward. Eyes now look at right hand (see figs. 54, 55).

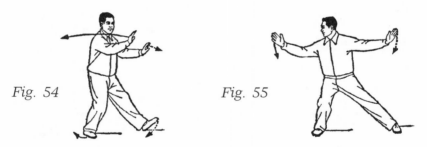

Fig. 54   *Fig. 55*

Movement 2: Slowly shift your weight onto the left leg, turn your right toes inward and draw back your right foot, keeping it shoulder-width apart from the left, and then gradually straighten both your legs with toes pointing forward. Meanwhile, both your hands descend past your abdomen in arc-like fashion, then travel inward and upward to cross each other in front of your chest, palm inward, right hand on the outside. Eyes now look horizontally forward (see figs. 56, 57).

Fig. 56

Fig. 57

Notes:

A. As your hands come into a crisscross, both your arms should be kept in an arc-shape with elbows slightly bent and shoulders hanging down.

B. When you straighten your legs, keep your body naturally erect, hold your chin slightly in, and avoid tensing any part of your body.

14. Carry Tiger to Mountain

Movement 1 (continued from fig. 57): With your weight slightly moving to the right foot, turn your left toes in, slowly bend both your legs at the knees, and shift your weight onto the left leg. At the same time, bring your left hand down to the left, then up in a curve until level with your left shoulder, palm diagonally upward, and begin to lower your right hand in front of your body, with palm down. Eyes now look at left hand (see fig. 58).

Fig. 58

Movement 2: Turn your upper body to the right, take a step to the right back corner with your right foot, and shift your weight onto it to form a right bow-shaped step. While doing so, bring your left hand back and push it past your left ear and forward, with palm outward and fingers at nose level; let your right hand continue to descend in a curve to the outside of your right thigh, palm downward. Eyes now look at left hand (see fig. 59).

Fig. 59

Notes:

A. In this posture, you are required to turn your upper body about 130 degrees to the right.

B. Synchronize turning your upper body right, pushing your left hand forward and forming a right bow-shaped step with your right leg.

15. Grasp the Bird's Tail in a Diagonal Way

Movement 1 (continued from fig. 59): Raise your right hand from the right side to shoulder-height, palm obliquely down, and let your left palm turn to face up and come near the wrist of your right hand. Then draw both hands downward, backward and upward to the left until the left hand is level with your left shoulder, palm upward, and the right hand is in front of your chest, palm inward. At the same time, shift your weight onto the left leg. Eyes now look at left hand (see figs. 60, 61).

Fig. 60

Fig. 61

Movement 2: Repeat Movement 6 of Posture 3 (see figs. 62, 63).

Fig. 62

Fig. 63

Movement 3: Repeat Movement 7 of Posture 3 (see fig. 64).

Fig. 64

Movement 4: Repeat Movement 8 of Posture 3 (see fig. 65).

Fig. 65

Notes are the same as mentioned in Posture 3.

16. Fist under Elbow

Movement 1 (continued from fig. 65): Draw your upper body back, move your weight onto the left leg, turn your right toes in and your upper body to the left. While turning your body, bring both hands (the left higher than the right) across your chest to the left, until the left arm holds horizontally on the left side of your body with palm facing slantingly downward, and the right arm lies in front of your left rib with palm facing upward. Eyes now look at left hand (see fig. 66).

Fig. 66

Movement 2: Shift your weight onto your right leg, draw your left foot close to the right. Meanwhile, move your right hand upward in a curve toward the upper right side of your body until it is about level with your shoulder, palm outward; let your left hand come down, across your abdomen and up in a curve to rest in front of your right shoulder, palm inward. Eyes now look at right hand (see fig. 67).

Fig. 67

Movement 3: Take a step to the left with your left foot, toes pointing outward; turn your body to the left and shift your weight onto the left leg. With the turning of your body, draw your right foot close to the left. At the same time, bring your left hand to the left side, then draw it back to place below your left rib, palm up, and let your right hand also go left in a curve to rest in front of your chest. Eyes now look forward (see figs. 68, 69).

Fig. 68   Fig. 69

Notes:

A. Do not move your right foot forward until your left foot stands firm.

B. Both your arms should move to the left in conjunction with your waist.

Movement 4: Let your left hand rise from the left side, cross over the wrist of your right hand and go forward until it is level with your nose, palm facing right. Turn your right hand into a fist and let it remain under the elbow of your left arm with fist hole (formed by the thumb and index finger) facing upward. In the meantime, shift your weight onto the right leg, and take a small step forward with the left leg, heel on the ground, knee slightly bent, forming a left empty step. Eyes now look at the forefinger of the left hand (see fig. 70).

Fig. 70

Notes:

A. Keep your upper body upright and do not throw out your buttocks.

B. Make sure that your weight is on your right leg when you extend your left palm forward.

17. Step Back to Drive the Monkey Away (Left and Right)

Movement 1 (continued from fig. 70): Open your right fist, palm up, and move it downward and backward in a curve, past your right thigh and up to shoulder-height, palm still up. At the same time, turn your left palm to face up, and move your left foot back with only the toes touching the ground. Eyes now look at left hand (see figs. 71, 72).

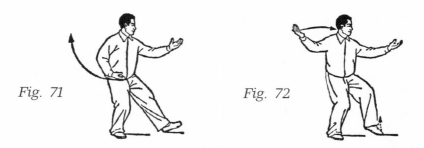

Fig. 71   Fig. 72

Movement 2: Bend your right elbow and push your right hand forward by the side of your right ear with palm facing forward. As your right hand moves forward, bring your left hand downward and backward in a curve, past your left thigh, up to shoulder-height, palm still up. At the same time, take a step back with your left foot and shift your weight backward onto it, making your right foot an empty step. Meanwhile, turn your right palm to face up, and let your eyes look at it (see figs. 73, 74, 75).

Fig. 73   Fig. 74   Fig. 75

Movement 3: Bend your left elbow and push your left hand forward by the side of your left ear with palm facing forward. As your left hand moves forward, bring your right hand back in a curve past your right thigh and up to shoulder-height, palm up. At the same time, take a step back with your right foot, and shift your weight backward onto it, making your left foot an empty step. Meanwhile, turn your left palm to face up and let your eyes look at it (see figs. 76, 77, 78).

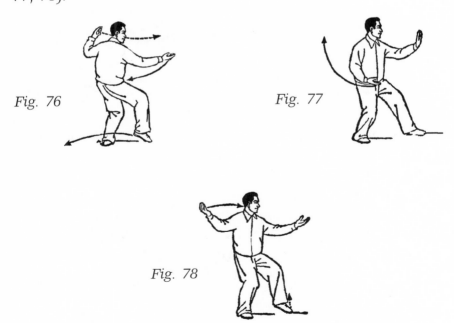

Fig. 76   Fig. 77

Fig. 78

Movement 4: Repeat Movement 2 (see figs. 79, 80, 81).

Fig. 79

Fig. 80

Fig. 81

Notes:

A. Do not straighten your arm when pushing your hand forward; do not draw your front hand backward in a straight line, but in a curve.

B. When you step back, let the toes of your foot touch the ground first. In the meantime, turn your front foot on the toes.

C. When you step back with your left foot, the left foot should be moved backward slightly to the left, and when you step back with your right foot, the right foot should be moved backward slightly to the right, only thus can you maintain good balance and make your steps steady.

D. When you step back, your eyes should first look in the direction of your body's turn and then at your front hand.

18. *Diagonal Flying Posture*

Movement 1 (continued from fig. 81): Turn your upper body slightly to the left, bring both your hands together to form a holding-ball position in front of your left chest, with the left hand above the right. At the same time, draw your right foot close to the inside of the left foot, toes on the ground (see fig. 82).

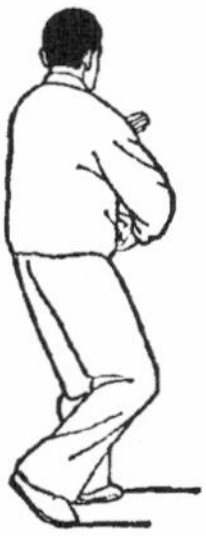

Fig. 82

Movement 2: Turn your body right, take a step forward to the right with your right foot, and shift your weight onto it to assume a right bow-shaped step. At the same time, separate your hands—the right hand moving right and up to eye-level, palm slantingly upward; the left hand descending to the side of your left hip, palm down with fingers pointing forward. Eyes now look at right hand (see figs. 83, 84).

Fig. 83    *Fig. 84*

Notes:

A. In order to maintain good balance, you must turn your body slowly and smoothly to the right.

B. Coordinate extending your right hand forward with forming a right bow-shaped step with your right leg.

19. Lifting Hands

Movements (continued from fig. 84): Take a half step forward with your left foot and shift your weight onto it, then lift your right foot and let it alight again with heel touching the ground and knee slightly bent, forming a right empty step. As you do so, your right hand moves from the right side to rest in front of your face with palm facing left and being level with eyebrow; your left hand comes near the inside of your right arm, palm facing right and about chest-height. Eyes now look at the forefinger of right hand (see figs. 85, 86).

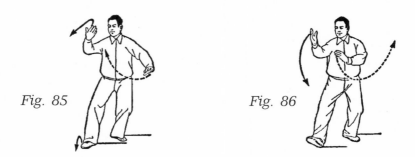

Fig. 85   Fig. 86

Notes are the same as mentioned in Posture 5.

20. White Crane Spreads Its Wings

Both movements and notes are the same as mentioned in Posture 6 (see figs. 87, 88, 89).

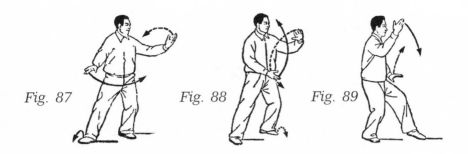

Fig. 87   Fig. 88   Fig. 89

21. Brush Left Knee and Twist Step

Both movements and notes are the same as mentioned in Posture 7 (see figs. 90, 91, 92, 93).

Fig. 90   Fig. 91

Fig. 92   Fig. 93

22. Needle at Sea Bottom

To complete this posture you are asked to act as if fishing for a needle from the bottom of the sea.

Movements (continued from fig. 93): Draw your right foot close to the heel of the left foot, shift your weight back onto the right leg which now slightly bends at the knee; then move your left foot a little forward with toes touching the ground, forming a left empty step. At the same time, bring your right hand down, back and up in a curve to the side of your right ear, then drop it down in front of your body with fingers pointing downward. Circle your left hand on the left side of your body and then let it return to the side of your left hip again. Eyes now look slantingly downward (see figs. 94, 95).

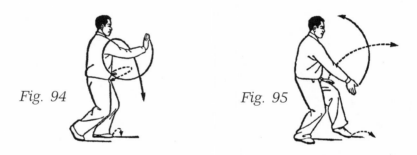

Fig. 94   Fig. 95

Notes:

A. Avoid bowing your head, protruding your buttocks or pulling your shoulder down while your right hand is dropping.

B. Your weight is on your right leg, and your left leg should be moderately bent at the knee.

C. At the end of the posture, your upper body should not lean too far forward.

23. *Fend Off and Push Away with Arms*

Movements (continued from fig. 95): Turn your upper body slightly to the right, take a small step forward with the left leg, and shift your weight onto it to assume a left bow-shaped step. As you do so, raise your right hand in front of your body in a curve to lie above your forehead with palm facing obliquely outward, so that your right arm comes into a semicircle; let your left hand push out horizontally in front of your chest, with palm facing forward and being level with the tip of your nose. Eyes now look at left hand (see fig. 96).

Fig. 96

Notes:

A. Keep your upper body erect in a natural state with waist and hips relaxed.

B. Do not straighten your left arm when you push it out.

C. Keep your shoulders sunk and your back muscles fully stretched.

D. Synchronize your weight shift with the movements of your arms and legs.

24. Turn, Deflect, and Punch

Movement 1 (continued from fig. 96): Slowly bend your right leg to shift your weight back onto it and turn your left toes in; turn your body right, then shift your weight onto the left leg again. With the turning of the body, move your right hand right, down (turning into a fist now), and across your abdomen in a curve to rest by the side of your left rib, the back of the fist upward; raise your left hand in a curve to lie above the forehead with palm facing diagonally upward and arm being like a bow. Eyes now look forward (see fig. 97).

Fig. 97

Movement 2: Continue to turn your body right, take a step forward to the right with your right foot, shift your weight onto it to assume a right bow-shaped step. At the same time, throw out your right fist to the right, the back of the fist downward; let your left hand come down to the inside of your right elbow. Eyes now look at right fist (see fig. 98).

Fig. 98

Notes:

A. Draw your right foot back (without touching the ground), and then step forward to the right with it.

B. Synchronize throwing out your right fist to the right with shifting your weight onto your right foot.

25. *Step Forward, Intercept, and Punch*

Movement 1 (continued from fig. 98): Bend your left leg, shift your weight onto it, and draw your right foot back to the inside of the left foot, toes on the ground. Meanwhile, turn your right fist over (the back of the fist up) and let it go down, left and across your abdomen in a curve to lie below your left rib; bring your left hand a little back to lie in front of your chest, palm down (see fig. 99).

Fig. 99

Movement 2: Step forward with your right foot with toes pointing outward. At the same time, throw out your right fist across your chest in a curve, the back of the fist down; let your left hand descend to the side of your left hip, palm down. Eyes now look horizontally forward (see fig. 100).

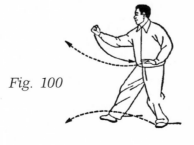

Fig. 100

Movement 3: Shift your weight forward onto the right leg, bring your right fist to the right side of your waist, the back of your fist downward, and stretch out your left hand from the left side to assume an intercepting position. At the same time, take a step forward with the left foot, and move your weight onto it to form a left bow-shaped step. While doing so, punch your right fist forward at chest level, with fist hole upward, and let your left hand attach to the inside of the right forearm. Eyes now look at right fist (see figs. 101, 102).

Fig. 101   Fig. 102

Notes are the same as mentioned in Posture 11.

26. Step Forward to Grasp the Bird's Tail

Movement 1 (continued from fig. 102): Shift your weight slightly backward, turn your body a little to the left and turn your left toes outward. As you do so, let your left hand go down, left, back and up in a curve to rest in front of your chest, palm down, and your right fist change into an open palm, then come back and down in a curve to lie in front of your abdomen, palm up, forming a holding-ball position. Meanwhile, bring your right foot forward to the inside of the left foot, toes on the ground. Eyes now look at left hand (see fig. 103).

Fig. 103

Movement 2: Repeat Movement 4 of Posture 3 (see fig. 104).

Fig. 104

Movement 3: Repeat Movement 5 of Posture 3 (see figs. 105, 106, 107).

Fig. 105

Fig. 106

Fig. 107

Movement 4: Repeat Movement 6 of Posture 3 (see figs. 108, 109).

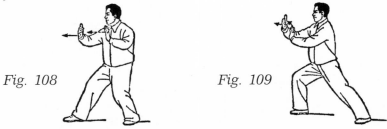

Fig. 108   *Fig. 109*

Movement 5: Repeat Movement 7 of Posture 3 (see figs. 110, 111, 112).

Fig. 110   *Fig. 111*

Fig. 112

Movement 6: Repeat Movement 8 of Posture 3 (see fig. 113).

Fig. 113

Notes are the same as mentioned in Posture 3.

27. *Single Whip*

Both movements and notes are the same as mentioned in Posture 4 (see figs. 114–118).

Fig. 114   Fig. 115

Fig. 116   Fig. 117   Fig. 118

28. *Wave Hands like Clouds*

Movement 1 (continued from fig. 118): Shift your weight onto the right foot, move your left toes inward, and turn your upper body gradually to the right. While doing so, let your left hand move across your abdomen and up to rest in front of your right shoulder, palm inclined inward; let your right hand change from the beaked hand into an open palm (facing outward). Eyes now look at left hand (see figs. 119, 120).

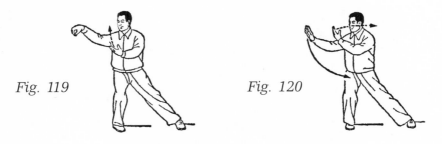

Fig. 119   Fig. 120

Movement 2: Slowly shift your weight onto the left foot, move your left hand across your face to the left side with palm turning gradually to the left, and bring your right hand down, across the abdomen and up to rest in front of your left shoulder, palm inclined inward. At the same time, draw your right foot closer to the left, and keep them parallel to each other and 4—5 inches apart. Eyes now look at right hand (see figs. 121, 122).

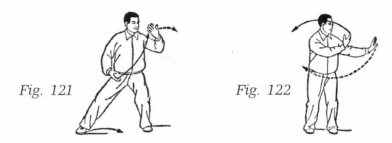

Fig. 121 *Fig. 122*

Movement 3: Shift your weight onto the right foot, move your right hand across your face to the right side with palm turning gradually to the right, and bring your left hand down, across your abdomen and up to rest in front of your right shoulder, palm inclined inward. At the same time, turn your right palm to the right and take a side step to the left with the left foot. Eyes now look at left hand (see figs. 123, 124).

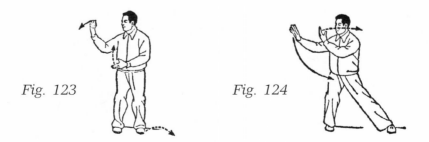

Fig. 123 *Fig. 124*

Movement 4: Repeat Movement 2 (see figs. 125, 126).

Fig. 125   Fig. 126

Movement 5: Repeat Movement 3 (see figs. 127, 128).

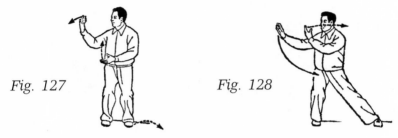

Fig. 127   Fig. 128

Movement 6: Repeat Movement 2 (see figs. 129, 130).

Fig. 129   Fig. 130

Notes:

A. Take your lumbar spine as the axis when turning your body, move your arms along with the turn in your waist, and let your eyes follow the hand crossing your face.

B. As you take sidesteps, move your legs slowly and steadily, pay attention to keeping your balance and avoiding up-and-down actions.

C. Keep your waist and hips relaxed, and do not pull your shoulders up when moving your arms.

D. The movements of your arms should be natural and round, and at an even speed.

29. Single Whip

Movement 1 (continued from fig. 130): Move your right hand in a curve to the upper right side and let it turn into a beaked hand; bring your left hand down, across your abdomen and up to rest in front of your right shoulder, palm inward. While doing so, shift your weight onto the right foot, and draw your left foot near the right, toes on the ground. Eyes now look at the left hand (see figs. 131, 132).

Fig. 131   *Fig. 132*

Movement 2: Turn your upper body slightly left, take a step forward to the left with your left foot, and shift your weight onto it to assume a left bow-shaped step. At the same time, turn your left palm outward and push it out to the left with fingers being level with your eyes. Let both your arms bend slightly to keep your shoulders sinking and elbows drooping. Eyes now look at left hand (see fig. 133).

Fig. 133

Notes are the same as mentioned in Posture 4.

30. Stroke the Horse from Above

Movement 1 (continued from fig. 133): Draw your right foot closer to the left while changing your right beaked hand into an open palm and turning both palms to face upward with elbows bending slightly. At the same time, turn your body slightly to the right, shift your weight back onto the right leg, and lift your left heel to form a left empty step. Eyes now look at left hand (see fig. 134).

Fig. 134

Movement 2: Push your right hand forward by the side of the right ear, palm facing forward, fingers at eyebrow level; bring your left hand back to the left side of your waist, palm facing upward. Eyes now look at right hand (see fig. 135).

Fig. 135

Notes:

A. When shifting your weight onto the right foot and assuming an empty step with the left foot, keep your upper body upright and do not protrude your buttocks.

B. Push your right hand forward in a curve, with elbows slightly bent and fingers pointing up.

31. Separate Right Foot

Movement 1 (continued from fig. 135): Raise your left hand in front of your chest with palm upward, and let it overpass the wrist of your right hand, so that your forearms make an "x-shape." Then separate your hands and let them go down and round in a circle to form crossing-hands in front of your chest, both palms inward, the right hand outside the left. At the same time, step forward with the left foot and shift your weight onto it to form a left bow-shaped step; draw your right foot forward to the inside of the left foot, toes on the ground. Eyes now look toward the right (see figs. 136, 137, 138).

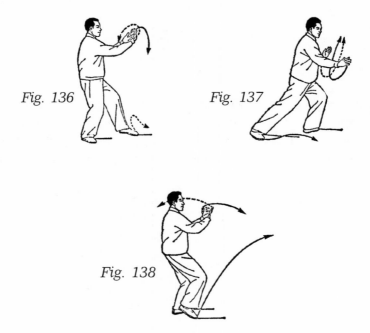

Fig. 136

Fig. 137

Fig. 138

Movement 2: Let your arms move apart from each other horizontally to both sides of your body with elbows slightly bent, palms facing outward. Meanwhile, lift up your right leg and gently stretch out in line with your right arm, toes pointing forward. Eyes now look at right hand (see fig. 139).

Fig. 139

Notes:

A. Your upper body should remain steady; neither bend forward nor lean backward.

B. Your wrists should be level with your shoulders when your arms are separated to both sides.

C. Your left leg should be slightly bent as your right leg stretches out.

D. At the conclusion, your right arm should be corresponding to your right leg in position.

32. *Separate Left Foot*

Movement 1 (continued from fig. 139): Bring your right leg back (just bending at the knee), then take a step forward with it, and shift your weight onto it to form a right bow-shaped step. Turn your body slightly right; let your left hand move across your chest and overpass the right wrist, palm upward. Then separate your hands and let them go down and round in a circle to form crossing-hands in front of your chest, both palms inward, the left hand outside the right. At the same time, bring your left foot forward to the inside of the right foot, toes on the ground. Eyes now look toward the left (see figs. 140, 141).

Fig. 140

Fig. 141

Movement 2: Let your arms move apart from each other horizontally to both sides of your body with elbows slightly bent, palms facing outward. Meanwhile, lift up your left leg and gently stretch out in line with your left arm, toes pointing forward. Eyes now look at left hand (see fig. 142).

Fig. 142

Notes are the same as mentioned in Posture 31, only the related left and right are reversed.

33. Turn Round and Kick With Left Heel

This posture is ended in a position of striking with your heel rather than toes. It is actually more like a "push" with your foot than what is usually called a "kick."

Movement 1 (continued from fig. 142): Bring your left foot back to alight behind the right, toes on the ground, and, pivoting on the heel of the right foot, turn your body gradually to the left about 180 degrees. In the meantime, bring both your hands back to cross each other in front of your chest, palms inward. Eyes now look obliquely toward the left (see figs. 143, 144).

Fig. 143

Fig. 144

Movement 2: Let your arms move apart from each other horizontally to both sides of your body with wrists at shoulder level, elbows slightly bent, and palms facing outward. At the same time, lift up your left foot and gently kick out to the left, heel leading toes. Your left arm and left leg now come into an overlapping position, leg below the arm. Eyes now look at left hand (see fig. 145).

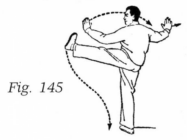

Fig. 145

Notes:

A. Do not let your upper body lean either forward or backward in order to maintain good balance.

B. Synchronize separating your hands with extending your left foot out.

C. Your right leg should be slightly bent as your left foot kicks out.

D. Make sure that the left toes are drawn back while kicking out with the left foot.

E. At the end of the posture, your left arm should be vertically parallel to your left leg.

34. Brush Knee and Twist Step (Left and Right)

Movement 1 (continued from fig. 145): Let your left foot alight, then step forward with it and move your weight onto it to form a left bow-shaped step. As you do so, bring your left hand back to lie in front of your right shoulder, palm down; turn your right palm upward and push it out by the side of your right ear. Meanwhile, your left hand drops down and brushes past your left knee to rest beside your left hip. Eyes now look at the forefinger of right hand (see figs. 146, 147).

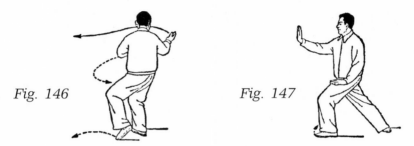

Fig. 146   *Fig. 147*

Movement 2: Repeat Movement 3 of Posture 9 (see figs. 148, 149, 150).

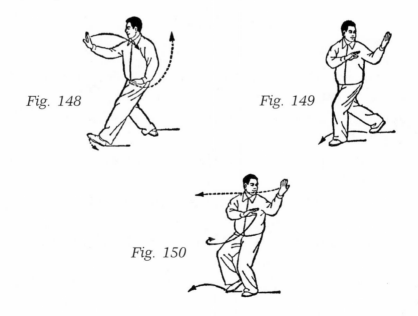

Fig. 148   *Fig. 149*

Fig. 150

Movement 3: Repeat Movement 4 of Posture 9 (see fig. 151).

Fig. 151

35. Step Forward and Punch Down with Fist

Movements (continued from fig. 151): Shift your weight slightly backward, turn your right toes outward and your body to the right. With the turning of your body, your left hand comes back to rest in front of your right shoulder, palm down, and your right hand rises up from behind in a curve and turns into a fist. Now move your weight forward and draw your left foot close to the inside of the right foot. Then take a step forward with your left foot and shift your weight onto it to form a left bow-shaped step. At the same time, your left hand drops down and brushes past your left knee to rest beside your left hip, palm down; your right fist punches down in front of your body, the back of the fist outward. Eyes now look diagonally downward (see figs. 152, 153, 154).

Fig. 152   Fig. 153   Fig. 154

Notes:

A. Keep your upper body erect, your waist and hips relaxed.

B. As punching down with your right fist, your right shoulder should not lean downward.

36. White Snake Puts Out Its Tongue

Movement 1 (continued from fig. 154): Shift your weight back onto the right leg, lift up your right fist and raise your left hand to the front of your forehead. Turn your left toes in, turn your body to the right, and shift your weight onto the left leg again. Draw your right foot back, then step forward with it. In the meantime, throw out your right fist in line with your right leg, the back of the fist downward; lower your left hand to rest in front of your abdomen, palm down. Eyes now look at right fist (see figs. 155, 156, 157, 158).

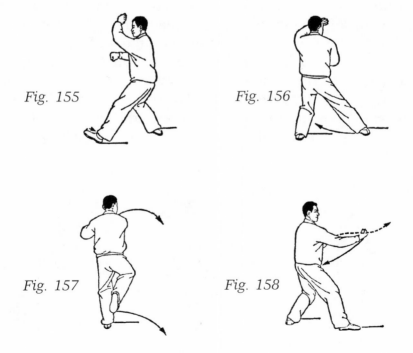

Fig. 155

Fig. 156

Fig. 157

Fig. 158

Movement 2: Extend your left hand forward and across your right fist, palm outward. At the same time, bow your right leg to form a right bow-shaped step; let your right fist turn into an open palm and retract to the right side of your waist, palm up. Eyes now look at left hand (see fig. 159).

Fig. 159

Movement 3: Shift your weight back onto the left leg, and draw your right foot a little backward with heel slightly raised, assuming a right empty step. While doing this, change your right hand into a fist, and punch forward from below the left hand with the hole of the fist facing upward; attach your left hand to the inside of the right forearm. Eyes now look at right fist (see fig. 160).

Fig. 160

Notes:

A. Your upper body should be kept upright.

B. Do not straighten your right arm while punching forward with your right fist.

C. Your left hand should move in a curve whether extending forward or drawing backward.

37. *Step Forward, Intercept, and Punch*

Movement 1 (continued from fig. 160): Turn your body to the left, draw your right foot near the left, toes on the ground. Meanwhile, bring both your right fist and left palm to the left side of your waist, palm downward, the back of the fist upward (see fig. 161).

Fig. 161

Movement 2: Repeat Movement 2 of Posture 11 (see fig. 162).

Fig. 162

Movement 3: Repeat Movement 3 of Posture 11 (see fig. 163).

Fig. 163

Movement 4: Repeat Movement 4 of Posture 11 (see fig. 164).

Fig. 164

Notes are the same as mentioned in Posture 11.

38. Kick with Right Heel

Movement 1 (continued from fig. 164): Turn your right fist into an open palm, then separate your hands and let them go down on both sides of your body and round in a circle to finally cross in front of your chest, both palms inward, the right hand outside the left. At the same time, move your weight a little backward and turn your left toes slightly outward, then let your weight return to the left leg and bring your right foot to the inside of the left foot, toes on the ground. Eyes now look forward to the right (see figs. 165, 166).

Fig. 165

Fig. 166

Movement 2: Let your arms move apart from each other horizontally to both sides of your body with elbows slightly bent, palms facing outward. At the same time, lift your right leg and gently kick out in line with your right arm, heel leading toes. Eyes now look at right hand (see fig. 167).

Fig. 167

Notes are the same as mentioned in Posture 33, only the related left and right are reversed.

39. Sway Body to the Left to Subdue the Tiger

Movement 1 (continued from fig. 167): Draw your right foot back to alight behind the left, assuming a crisscross step. Meanwhile, bring your left hand down from the upper left side in a curve to the inside of your right forearm. Eyes now look at right hand (see fig. 168).

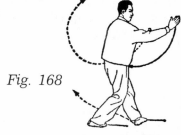

Fig. 168

Movement 2: Take a step to the left with your left foot. While doing so, turn your body to the left about 90 degrees, and shift your weight onto the left leg to assume a left bow-shaped step. At the same time, bring both your hands down, across your abdomen and up in a curve: the right hand turning into a fist and resting in front of your left chest with fist back upward; the left hand turning into a fist and lying in front of your left temple with fist back inward. Now your fists are vertically opposite each other. Your eyes now look toward the right (see fig. 169).

Fig. 169

Notes:

A. Relax your chest muscles when your fists come into the position as if you were subduing a tiger.

B. At the end of the posture, both your arms should be kept in an arc-shape.

40. Sway Body to the Right to Subdue the Tiger

Movements (continued from fig. 169): Shift your weight back onto the right leg and turn your left toes in, then let your weight return to the left leg. Lift your right foot to take a step to the right and make a right bow-shaped step. In company with these movements, change both your fists into open palms, and let them go down, across your abdomen and up in a curve: the left palm turning into a fist again and resting in front of your right chest with fist back upward, the right palm also turning into a fist and resting in front of your right temple with fist back inward. Now your fists are vertically opposite each other. Your eyes now look toward the left (see figs. 170, 171, 172).

Fig. 170   Fig. 171   Fig. 172

Notes are the same as mentioned in Posture 39.

41. Withdraw and Kick with Right Heel

Movement 1 (continued from fig. 172): Bend your left leg, shift your weight onto it, turn your right toes inward and your body to the left. Let both fists change into open palms and separate in front of your face to make circles and finally cross each other in front of your chest, palms inward, the right outside the left. In the meantime, draw your right foot close to the inside of the left foot, toes on the ground. Eyes now look forward to the right (see figs. 173, 174, 175).

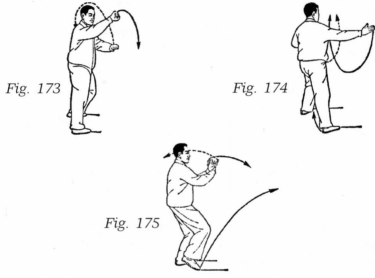

Fig. 173

Fig. 174

Fig. 175

Movement 2: Repeat Movement 2 of Posture 38 (see fig. 176).

Fig. 176

Notes are the same as mentioned in Posture 33, only the related left and right are reversed.

42. Hit the Opponent's Ears with Both Fists

Movement 1 (continued from fig. 176): Bend your right leg at the knee, keeping the thigh parallel to the ground and the toes pointing downward. Bring your left hand close to the right, then let both hands descend to the sides of your right knee, palms upward (see fig. 177).

Fig. 177

Movement 2: Let your right foot fall on the ground, and shift your weight onto it to form a right bow-shaped step. At the same time, turn both your hands into fists, and let them separate to both sides, moving forward and round in a circle to form a pincer-like shape in front of you, at eye level, with fist holes (formed by the thumb and index finger of each hand) facing obliquely downward. The distance between fists should be about 6 inches. Eyes now look at right fist (see figs. 178, 179).

Fig. 178   *Fig. 179*

Notes:

A. Hold your head and neck upright, relax your chest and waist, and keep your shoulders sunk and elbows drooped during the whole process.

B. Do not clench your fists tightly, but rather loosely.

C. At the conclusion of the posture, both your arms should be kept in an arc-shape.

43. Kick with Left Heel

Movement 1 (continued from fig. 179): Shift your weight back onto the left leg, and turn your right toes out. Change both your fists into open palms, and separate them to both sides to make circles and finally cross each other in front of your chest, both palms inward, the left outside the right. In the meantime, move your weight onto the right leg again, and draw your left foot forward to the inside of the right foot, toes on the ground. Eyes now look slightly toward the left (see figs. 180, 181).

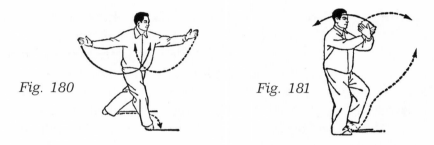

Fig. 180   *Fig. 181*

Movement 2: Repeat Movement 2 of Posture 33 (see fig. 182).

Fig. 182

Notes are the same as mentioned in Posture 33.

44. Turn Round and Kick with Right Heel

Movement 1 (continued from fig. 182): Draw your left leg back (by bending at the knee) to the outside of the right leg and turn your body about 180 degrees to the right on your right toes. Let your weight fall on the left foot as soon as it alights on the ground, thus turning your right foot into a right empty step. Meanwhile, bring both your hands down and round in a curve to cross each other in front of your chest, both palms inward, the right hand outside the left. Eyes now look obliquely toward the right (see figs. 183, 184).

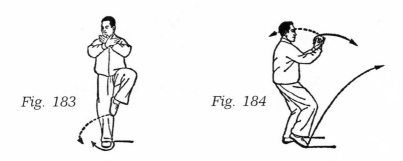

Fig. 183   *Fig. 184*

Movement 2: Repeat Movement 2 of Posture 38 (see fig. 185).

Fig. 185

45. *Step Forward, Intercept, and Punch*

Movement 1 (continued from fig. 185): Bring your right foot down to the inside of the left foot, toes on the ground. In the meantime, turn your right palm into a fist and let it go down and across your abdomen to lie below your left rib, the back of the fist up; bring your left palm back to rest in front of your chest, palm down (see fig. 186).

Fig. 186

Movement 2: Repeat Movement 2 of Posture 25 (see fig. 187).

Fig. 187

Movement 3: Repeat Movement 3 of Posture 25 (see figs. 188, 189).

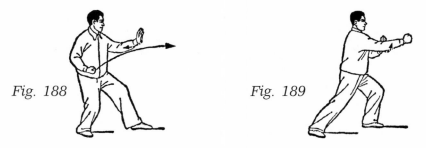

Fig. 188   *Fig. 189*

Notes are the same as mentioned in Posture 11.

46. As if Blocking and Closing

Both movements and notes are the same as mentioned in Posture 12 (see figs. 190–193).

Fig. 190

Fig. 191

Fig. 192

Fig. 193

47. Cross Hands

Both movements and notes are the same as mentioned in Posture 13 (see figs. 194–197).

Fig. 194

Fig. 195

Fig. 196

Fig. 197

48. Carry Tiger to Mountain

Both movements and notes are the same as mentioned in Posture 14 (see figs. 198, 199).

Fig. 198

Fig. 199

49. Grasp the Bird's Tail in a Diagonal Way

Both movements and notes are the same as mentioned in Posture 15 (see figs. 200–205).

Fig. 200

Fig. 201

Fig. 202

Fig. 203

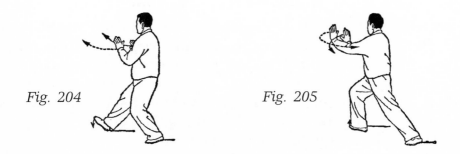

Fig. 204

Fig. 205

50. Sideways Single Whip

Repeat all the movements of Posture 4, the only difference is that when you step out with the left foot to make a left bow-shaped step, you are asked to step to the front by left, not to the left (see figs. 206–209).

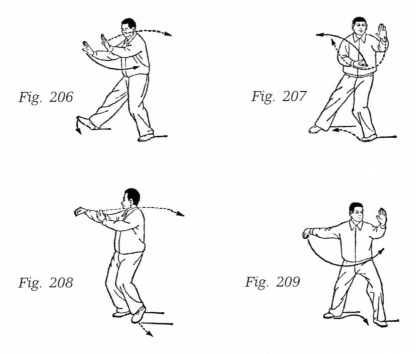

Fig. 206

Fig. 207

Fig. 208

Fig. 209

Notes are the same as mentioned in Posture 4.

51. *Wild Horse Waves Its Mane (Left and Right)*

Movement 1 (continued from fig. 209): Turn your body slightly to the left, bring your left hand back to rest in front of your chest, palm down, and turn your right beaked hand into an open palm and let it travel down to the right to lie below the left hand, palm up, so that your hands are in the holding-ball position. Meanwhile, bring your right foot close to the inside of the left foot, toes on the ground. Eyes now look at left hand (see fig. 210).

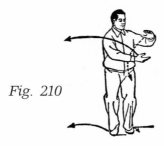

Fig. 210

Movement 2: Take a step forward to the right with your right foot, and shift your weight onto it to make a right bow-shaped step. At the same time, let your hands separate—the right hand goes right and up to eye-level, palm obliquely upward; the left hand descends to the side of your left hip, palm down. Eyes now look at right palm (see fig. 211).

Fig. 211

Movement 3: Draw your upper body back to shift your weight onto the left leg, and move your right toes slightly outward.

Then turn your body to the right and shift your weight onto the right leg to form a right bow-shaped step. At the same time, bring your right hand back to rest in front of your chest, palm down; move your left hand across your abdomen to the right to lie below the right hand, palm up, so that your hands are in the holding-ball position. While doing so, draw your left foot close to the inside of the right foot, toes on the ground. Eyes now look at right hand (see figs. 212, 213, 214).

Fig. 212   Fig. 213

Fig. 214

Movement 4: Practice according to Movement 2, but with opposite hands and feet (see fig. 215).

Fig. 215

Movement 5: Practice according to Movement 3, but with opposite hands and feet (see figs. 216, 217, 218).

Fig. 216

Fig. 217

Fig. 218

Movement 6: Repeat Movement 2 (see fig. 219).

Fig. 219

Notes:

A. Your upper body should be kept upright, not leaning forward or backward, and its turning should always pivot on your waist.

B. Your chest should be fully relaxed and both your arms should remain in an arc-shape when your hands go apart from each other.

C. The parting of hands and the assuming of a bow-shaped step should be done in a coordinated way and an even pace.

D. In forming a bow-shaped step, do not bend your knee beyond the toes of the foot.

52. Step Forward to Grasp the Bird's Tail

Movement 1 (continued from fig. 219): Draw your body back to shift your weight onto the left leg, and turn your right toes slightly outward. Then shift your weight onto the right leg to form a right bow-shaped step; turn your body slightly to the right. Simultaneously, bring your right hand back to rest in front of your chest, palm down, and move your left hand across your abdomen in a curve to lie below the right hand, palm up, forming a holding-ball position. As you do so, draw your left foot close to the inside of the right foot, toes on the ground. Eyes now look at the right hand (see figs. 220, 221, 222).

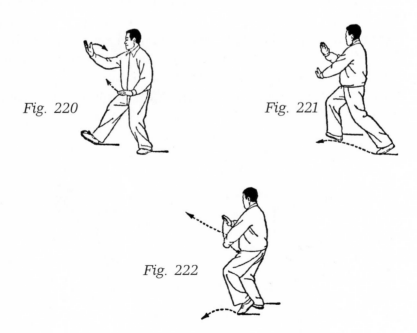

Fig. 220

Fig. 221

Fig. 222

Movement 2: Take a step to the left with your left foot, and shift your weight onto it to make a left bow-shaped step. In the meantime, separate your hands: the left goes to the upper left at shoulder level, palm inward, and the right descends to the side of your right hip, palm downward. Eyes now look at left forearm (see fig. 223).

Fig. 223

Movement 3: Draw your body back to shift your weight onto the right leg, turn your left toes outward (about 45 degrees) and your upper body slightly to the left. Bring your left hand back to rest in front of your chest, palm down, and move your right hand across your abdomen in a curve to lie below the left hand, palm up, forming a holding-ball position. Meanwhile, draw your right foot close to the inside of the left foot, toes on the ground. Eyes now look at left hand (see figs. 224, 225).

Fig. 224

Fig. 225

Movement 4: Repeat Movement 4 of Posture 3 (see fig. 226).

Fig. 226

Movement 5: Repeat Movement 5 of Posture 3 (see figs. 227, 228, 229).

Fig. 227   *Fig. 228*   *Fig. 229*

Movement 6: Repeat Movement 6 of Posture 3 (see figs. 230, 231).

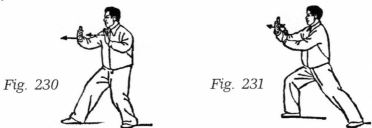

Fig. 230   *Fig. 231*

Movement 7: Repeat Movement 7 of Posture 3 (see figs. 232, 233).

Fig. 232   *Fig. 233*

Movement 8: Repeat Movement 8 of Posture 3 (see fig. 234).

Fig. 234

Notes are the same as mentioned in Posture 3.

53. Single Whip

Both movements and notes are the same as mentioned in Posture 4 (see figs. 235–239).

Fig. 235

Fig. 236

Fig. 237

Fig. 238

Fig. 239

54. *Fair Lady Works with Shuttles*

This posture requests you to act as if a fair lady working with shuttles back and forth on the loom. It is completed by doing similar movements at four oblique corners. If you start your practice facing south, you will perform the posture at 1) south-west corner, 2) south-east corner, 3) north-east corner and 4) north-west corner.

Movement 1 (continued from fig. 239): Shift your weight slightly back onto the right leg, and turn your left toes in (about 130 degrees). Then shift your weight onto the left leg, turn your right toes out (about 130 degrees) and turn your body about 180 degrees to the right at the same time. Change your right beaked hand into an open palm and let it come back to lie in front of your right chest, palm downward; bring your left hand down and across your abdomen to rest below the right hand, palm upward, forming a holding-ball position with the right hand. Then take a step forward to the left with your left foot, and make a left bow-shaped step; at the same time, raise your left hand in a curve to lie above your forehead, palm diagonally upward, and push your right hand forward across your chest in a curve, holding at nose level, palm outward. Eyes now look at right hand (see figs. 240, 241, 242).

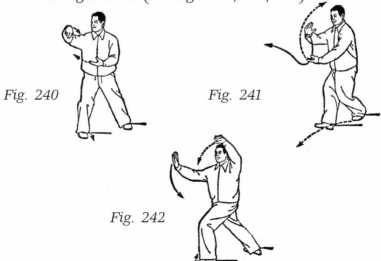

Fig. 240

Fig. 241

Fig. 242

Movement 2: Shift your weight onto the right leg, turn your left toes in (about 130 degrees). Then let your weight return to the left leg and turn your body about 180 degrees to the right with the right foot drawn beside the left, toes on the ground. In the meantime, bring both hands back to assume a holding-ball position in front of your left chest, the left hand above the right. Then lift your right foot and step out with it to the right to make a right bow-shaped step; raise your right hand in a curve past your face to lie above your forehead, palm obliquely upward; and push your left hand forward across your chest in a curve, at nose level, palm outward. Eyes now look at left hand (see figs. 243, 244, 245).

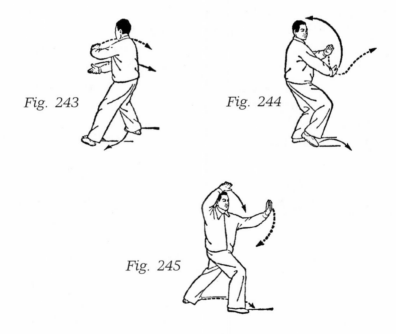

Fig. 243

Fig. 244

Fig. 245

Movement 3: Bring both your hands back to assume a holding-ball position in front of your right chest with the right hand above the left, turn your upper body slightly to the right, and draw your left foot close to the inside of the right foot. Then step forward to the left with your left foot to make a left bow-shaped step. In the meantime, raise your left hand in a curve past your face to lie above your forehead, palm diagonally upward, and push your right hand forward across your chest in a curve, at nose level, palm outward. Eyes now look at right hand (see figs. 246, 247).

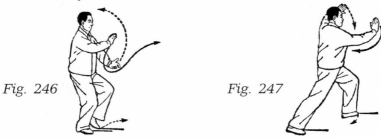

Fig. 246

Fig. 247

Movement 4: Practice according to Movement 2, but in the opposite direction (see figs. 248, 249, 250).

Fig. 248

Fig. 249

Fig. 250

Notes:

A. Avoid lifting your shoulders up when ֵ   your hanֵ
    to the forehead.

B. Do not lean forward with your upper body while push-
    ing your hand forward.

C. Coordinate pushing hand forward with bending your front
    leg and moving your upper body forward.

(These three points are applicable to either side.)

55. Step Forward to Grasp the Bird's Tail

Movement 1 (continued from fig. 250): Bring your hands
back to form a holding-ball position in front of your chest
with the right hand above the left, and draw your left foot
close to the inside of the right foot, toes on the ground. Eyes
now look at right hand (see fig. 251).

Fig. 251

Movement 2: Take a step to the left with your left foot, and
move your weight onto it to make a left bow-shaped step. At
the same time, separate your hands: the left rises up to the
upper left, at shoulder level, palm inward, and the right
descends to the side of your right hip, palm downward. Eyes
now look at left forearm (see fig. 252).

Fig. 252

Movement 3: Shift your weight a bit backward, turn your upper body slightly to the left and turn your left toes outward at the same time. As you do so , bring your left hand back to rest in front of your chest, palm downward; move your right hand across your abdomen to lie below the left hand, palm upward, forming a holding-ball position with the left hand; and draw your right foot close to the inside of the left foot, toes on the ground. Eyes now look at left hand (see fig. 253).

Fig. 253

Movement 4: Repeat Movement 4 of Posture 3 (see fig. 254).

Fig. 254

Movement 5: Repeat Movement 5 of Posture 3 (see figs. 255, 256, 257).

Fig. 255

Fig. 256

Fig. 257

Movement 6: Repeat Movement 6 of Posture 3 (see figs. 258, 259).

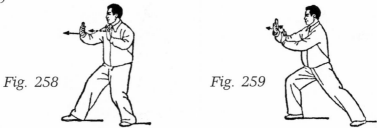

Fig. 258

Fig. 259

Movement 7: Repeat Movement 7 of Posture 3 (see figs. 260, 261).

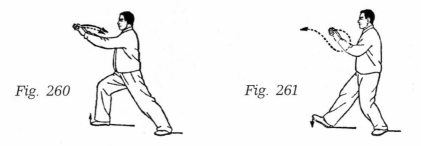

Fig. 260

Fig. 261

Movement 8: Repeat Movement 8 of Posture 3 (see fig. 262).

Fig. 262

Notes are the same as mentioned in Posture 3.

56. Single Whip

Both movements and notes are the same as mentioned in Posture 4 (see figs. 263–267).

Fig. 263   Fig. 264   Fig. 265

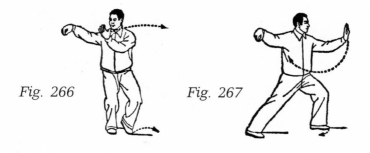

Fig. 266   Fig. 267

57. *Wave Hands like Clouds*

Both movements and notes are the same as mentioned in Posture 28 (see figs. 268–279).

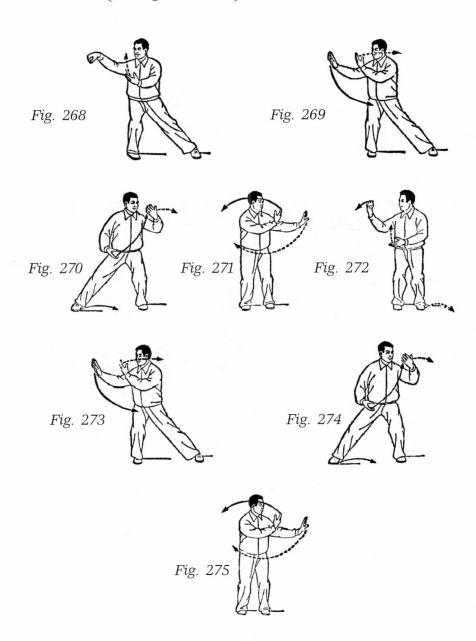

Fig. 268

Fig. 269

Fig. 270

Fig. 271

Fig. 272

Fig. 273

Fig. 274

Fig. 275

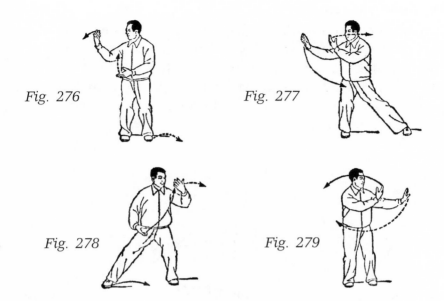

Fig. 276

Fig. 277

Fig. 278

Fig. 279

58. Single Whip

Repeat all the movements of Posture 29 (see figs. 280, 281, 282).

Fig. 280

Fig. 281

Fig. 282

Notes are the same as mentioned in Posture 4.

59. Squat Down

Movement 1 (continued from fig. 282): Keep your right beaked hand in the same position, shift your weight back onto the right leg, turn your upper body slightly to the right and turn your left toes in. Meanwhile, bring your left hand back to rest in front of your right armpit and let your eyes look at it (see fig. 283).

Fig. 283

Movement 2: Slowly squat down on your right leg, and extend your left leg as far as you can to the left to form a stretched step (usually called a "prostrating-step" in terms of Chinese martial arts). As you do so, let your left hand descend to your left thigh and then slide forward along the inside of your left leg. Eyes now look at left hand (see fig. 284).

Fig. 284

Notes:

A. As squatting down on your right leg, do not let your upper body lean too far forward.

B. In forming the stretched step with your left leg, try to straighten the leg as far as you can and keep the toes of the left foot slightly inward and the sole fully touching the ground.

60. Golden Cock Stands on One Leg (Left and Right)

Movement 1 (continued from fig. 284): Slowly straighten your right leg, turn your left toes out and right toes in, and shift your weight gradually forward onto the left leg. Then slowly lift your right leg, knee fully bent with toes downward. At the same time, open your right beaked hand into a palm and bring it forward and upward to shoulder level, with elbow above the right knee, palm facing left; lower your left hand to the side of your left hip, palm downward. Eyes now look at right hand. You are now in the posture of standing on one leg—the left leg (see figs. 285, 286).

Fig. 285   Fig. 286

Movement 2: Let your right foot alight behind the left, and slowly lift your left leg, knee fully bent with toes downward. At the same time, bring your left hand up to shoulder level, with elbow above the left knee, palm facing right; let your right hand descend to the side of your right hip, palm downward. Eyes now look at left hand. You are now in the posture of standing on one leg—the right leg (see fig. 287).

Fig. 287

Notes:

A. The standing leg should be slightly bent.

B. Keep your upper body upright and steady.

61. Step Back to Drive the Monkey Away (Left and Right)

Movement 1 (continued from fig. 287): Bring your right hand back in a curve past your right thigh and up to shoulder-height, palm up, then bend your right elbow and begin to push your right hand forward by the side of your right ear. As you do so, let your left foot alight in front of you with toes touching the ground, and lower your left arm a little, palm up, elbow slightly bent. Eyes now look at left hand (see fig. 288).

Fig. 288

Movement 2: Continue to push forward with your right hand, palm forward; bring your left hand back in a curve past your left thigh and up to shoulder-height, palm upward. As you complete this movement, take a step back with your left foot and shift your weight back onto it, making your right foot an empty step. In the meantime, turn your right palm to face up and let your eyes look at it (see figs. 289, 290).

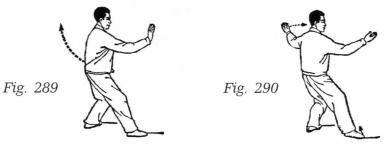

Fig. 289   *Fig. 290*

Movement 3: Repeat Movement 3 of Posture 17 (see figs. 291, 292, 293).

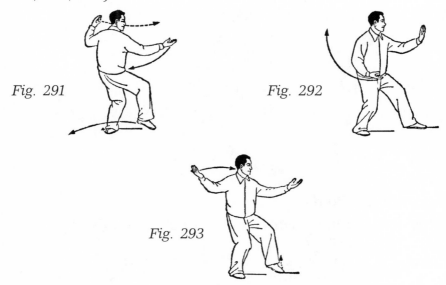

Fig. 291

Fig. 292

Fig. 293

Movement 4: Repeat Movement 2 of Posture 17 (see figs. 294, 295, 296).

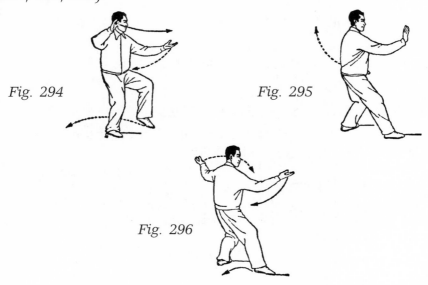

Fig. 294

Fig. 295

Fig. 296

Notes are the same as mentioned in Posture 17.

62. *Diagonal Flying Posture*

Both movements and notes are the same as mentioned in Posture 18 (see figs. 297, 298, 299).

Fig. 297   *Fig. 298*   *Fig. 299*

63. *Lifting Hands*

Repeat all the movements of Posture 19 (see figs. 300, 301).

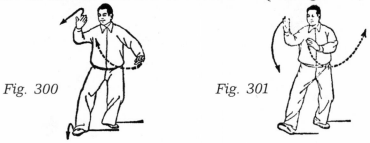

Fig. 300   *Fig. 301*

Notes are the same as mentioned in Posture 5.

64. *White Crane Spreads Its Wings*

Both movements and notes are the same as mentioned in Posture 6 (see figs. 302, 303, 304).

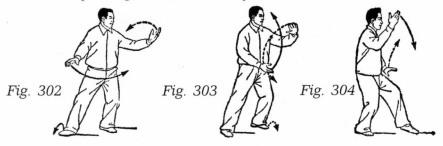

Fig. 302   *Fig. 303*   *Fig. 304*

65. Brush Left Knee and Twist Step

Both movements and notes are the same as mentioned in Posture 7 (see figs. 305–308).

Fig. 305

Fig. 306

Fig. 307

Fig. 308

66. Needle at Sea Bottom

Both movements and notes are the same as mentioned in Posture 22 (see figs. 309, 310).

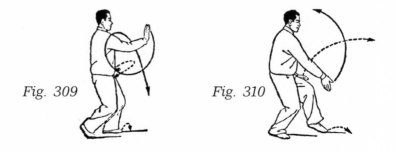

Fig. 309

Fig. 310

67. Fend Off and Push Away with Arms

Both movements and notes are the same as mentioned in Posture 23 (see fig. 311).

Fig. 311

68. Turn, Deflect, and Punch

Both movements and notes are the same as mentioned in Posture 24 (see figs. 312, 313).

Fig. 312   Fig. 313

69. Step Forward, Intercept, and Punch

Repeat all the movements of Posture 25 (see figs. 314–317).

Fig. 314   Fig. 315

Fig. 316   Fig. 317

Notes are the same as mentioned in Posture 11.

70. *Step Forward to Grasp the Bird's Tail*

Repeat all the movements of Posture 26 (see figs. 318–327).

Fig. 318   Fig. 319   Fig. 320

Fig. 321   Fig. 322   Fig. 323

Fig. 324   Fig. 325

Fig. 326   Fig. 327

Notes are the same as mentioned in Posture 3.

71. Single Whip

Both movement and notes are the same as mentioned in Posture 4 (see figs. 328–332).

Fig. 328

Fig. 329

Fig. 330

Fig. 331

Fig. 332

72. Wave Hands like Clouds

Both movements and notes are the same as mentioned in Posture 28 (see figs. 333–344).

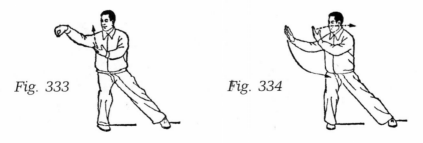

Fig. 333

Fig. 334

Fig. 335

Fig. 336

Fig. 337

Fig. 338

Fig. 339

Fig. 340

Fig. 341

Fig. 342

Fig. 343

Fig. 344

73. Single Whip

Repeat all the movements of Posture 29 (see figs. 345, 346, 347).

Fig. 345　　*Fig. 346*　　*Fig. 347*

Notes are the same as mentioned in Posture 4.

74. Stroke the Horse from Above

Both movements and notes are the same as mentioned in Posture 30 (see figs. 348, 349).

Fig. 348　　*Fig. 349*

75. Thrust with Left Palm

In practicing this posture, you are asked to act as if you were making a stab at your opponent's throat with your left palm.

Movements (continued from fig. 349): Raise your left palm in front of your chest, and let it stretch forward to cross the back of the right hand while your right hand is drawing back. In the meantime, take a small step forward with your left foot and shift your weight onto it to make a left bow-shaped step. Eyes now look at left palm (see fig. 350).

Fig. 350

Notes:

A. At the conclusion of the posture, your right hand should be under the left elbow, palm downward.

B. Your left palm should be at eye level with elbow slightly bent and palm obliquely upward when stretched out.

C. Synchronize extending your left palm with bowing your left leg and relaxing your waist.

76. *Turn Round, Cross Hands, and Kick with Right Heel*

Movement 1 (continued from fig. 350): Shift your weight onto the right leg and turn your left toes in. Then move your weight back to the left leg, turn your body 180 degrees to the right, and slightly raise your right heel, making your right foot an empty step. Along with the turning of the body, your hands travel in a curve to cross in front of your chest, both palms inward, right hand on the outside (see figs. 351, 352).

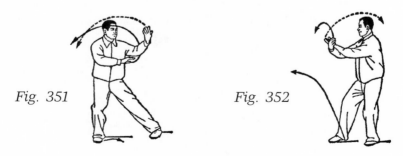

Fig. 351

Fig. 352

Movement 2: Separate your hands and extend them horizontally to both sides of your body with palms outward. At the same time, lift up your right foot and gently kick out with your heel. Eyes now look forward (see fig. 353).

Fig. 353

Notes:

A. Try to balance your body well while standing on one leg.

B. Your left leg should slightly bend at knee and get a firm foothold.

C. Extending your hands to both sides should coordinate with kicking out with your right heel.

77. *Brush Knee and Punch the Opponent on the Crotch*

Movement 1 (continued from fig. 353): Let your right foot alight in front of you with toes pointing slightly outward, turn your upper body a little to the right and move most of your weight onto the right leg. While doing so, let your right hand lower in a curve, turn into a fist and, with the turning of the body, draw to the side of your right hip, fist back downward; bring your left hand back in a curve to lie in front of your chest, palm downward. Eyes now look forward (see fig. 354).

Fig. 354

Movement 2: Step forward with your left foot to assume a left bow-shaped step and turn your body slightly to the left. At the same time, your left hand goes down and brushes past your left knee to rest beside your left hip, palm downward while your right fist punches forward, fist hole upward. Eyes now look forward (see fig. 355).

Fig. 355

Notes:

A. Do not lean forward or backward with your upper body.
B. When you punch forward with your right fist, do not straighten your right arm.
C. Your waist and hips should be kept relaxed.

78. Step Forward to Grasp the Bird's Tail

Movement 1 (continued from fig. 355): Shift your weight slightly back and turn your left toes out. Then change your right fist into an open palm and bring it back to lie in front of your abdomen, palm upward; circle your left hand out and up to rest in front of your chest, palm down, forming a holding-ball position with the right hand. Meanwhile, bring your right foot forward close to the inside of the left foot, toes on the ground. Eyes now look at left hand (see figs. 356, 357).

Fig. 356

Fig. 357

Movement 2: Repeat Movement 4 of Posture 3 (see fig. 358).

Fig. 358

Movement 3: Repeat Movement 5 of Posture 3 (see figs. 359, 360, 361).

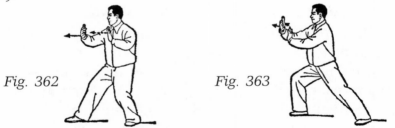

Fig. 359   Fig. 360   Fig. 361

Movement 4: Repeat Movement 6 of Posture 3 (see figs. 362, 363).

Fig. 362   Fig. 363

Movement 5: Repeat Movement 7 of Posture 3 (see figs. 364, 365).

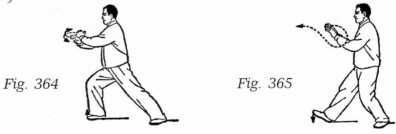

Fig. 364   Fig. 365

Movement 6: Repeat Movement 8 of Posture 3 (see fig. 366).

Fig. 366

Notes are the same as mentioned in Posture 3.

79. Single Whip

Both movements and notes are the same as mentioned in Posture 4 (see figs. 367–371).

Fig. 367

Fig. 368

Fig. 369

Fig. 370

Fig. 371

80. Squat Down

Both movements and notes are the same as mentioned in Posture 59 (see figs. 372, 373).

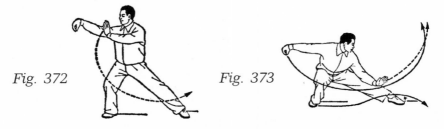

Fig. 372   Fig. 373

81. Step Up to Assume Seven Stars

Movements (continued from fig. 373): Turn your left toes slightly outward, move your weight gradually forward onto your left foot, erect your body and take a short step forward with your right foot, toes touching the ground, forming a right empty step. As you do so, both your right beaked hand and left palm turn into fists and rise up to form crossing-fists in front of your chest, fist back to fist back, the right fist outside the left. Eyes now look at both fists (see fig. 374).

Fig. 374

Notes:

A. When you form crossing-fists, your wrists should be kept close to each other, both your arms should assume an arc-like fashion, and your chest muscles should be fully relaxed.

B. Your right leg should be slightly bent at the knee.

82. Step Back to Mount the Tiger

Movements (continued from fig. 374): Step back a full step with your right foot and let your weight fall on it, meanwhile, draw your left foot back an inch or two to rest on its toes, forming a left empty step. As you do so, open both your fists into palms and let them separate: your right palm circles out and up to the right side of your body to lie in front of your head, palm outward, and your left palm descends in a curve to rest near the left side of your waist, palm obliquely outward. Eyes now look forward (see fig. 375).

Fig. 375

Notes:

A. Keep your shoulders at the same level.
B. Let your rear leg slightly bend to take the weight.
C. Slacken your chest muscles.

83. *Turn Round and Sweep Lotus with Foot*

Movement 1 (continued from fig. 375): Turn your body 180 degrees to the right. Along with the turning of the body, take a step forward with your left foot and shift your weight onto it to form a left bow-shaped step. At the same time, turn your left palm up and stretch it forward to overpass the wrist of the right hand which is drawing backward and, for the time being, to remain beneath the left elbow, palm downward. Eyes now look at left hand (see figs. 376, 377).

Fig. 376   *Fig. 377*

Movement 2: Shift your weight back to the right leg, turn your left toes in, and continue to turn your body to the right with your weight shifted onto your left leg. Lift up your right foot and sweep toward the upper right with leg naturally straightened, toes pointing forward. At the same time, bring both your hands across your face, then forward to slap the back of your right foot, the left hand leading the right. Eyes now look at right hand (see figs. 378, 379, 380).

Fig. 378

Fig. 379

Fig. 380

Notes:

A. When sweeping with your right foot, raise your right leg as high as possible and let your upper body lean slightly forward.

B. Do not force yourself to slap the back of your right foot if your hands cannot reach so far.

84. Bend the Bow and Shoot the Tiger

Movement 1 (continued from fig. 380): Let your right foot alight on the right side of your body and shift your weight onto it to make a right bow-shaped step. As you do so, bring both your hands across your body in a curve to the right side and change them into fists. Eyes now look toward the right (see figs. 381, 382).

Fig. 381   Fig. 382

Movement 2: Turn your upper body slightly to the left. At the same time, push your left fist forward to the left close to shoulder height, fist back obliquely inward; move your right fist from behind to the right side of your head about solar plexus height, fist back obliquely inward. The holes of the fists face each other, and both arms assume semicircles as if you were bending a bow and shooting something. Eyes now look at left fist (see fig. 383).

Fig. 383

Notes:

A. Keep your upper body upright and steady.

B. Your head should turn right along with the rightward moving of your hands, and your eyes should first look toward the right, then at your left fist.

C. At the conclusion of the posture, your left hand and arm should assume a pushing position and your right hand and arm, a drawing position.

85. Step Forward, Intercept, and Punch

Movement 1 (continued from fig. 383): Shift your weight onto the left leg, turn your body slightly to the left, and draw your right foot close to the inside of the left foot, toes on the ground. In the meantime, your right fist goes down in a curve to rest below your left rib, fist back upward, and your left fist opens into a palm and draws back in front of your chest, palm downward. Eyes now look at left hand (see figs. 384, 385).

Fig. 384   Fig. 385

Movement 2: Turn your body slightly to the right, throw out your right fist with its back facing downward, and lower your left palm to the side of your left hip, palm downward. Meanwhile, take a step forward with your right foot with toes pointing outward. Eyes now look at right fist (see fig. 386).

Fig. 386

Movement 3: Repeat Movement 3 of Posture 11 (see fig. 387).

Fig. 387

Movement 4: Repeat Movement 4 of Posture 11 (see fig. 388).

Fig. 388

Notes are the same as mentioned in Posture 11.

86. As if Blocking and Closing

Both movements and notes are the same as mentioned in Posture 12 (see figs. 389–392).

Fig. 389

Fig. 390

Fig. 391

Fig. 392

87. Cross Hands

Both movements and notes are the same as mentioned in Posture 13 (see figs. 393–396).

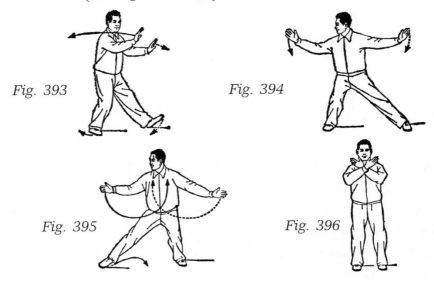

Fig. 393

Fig. 394

Fig. 395

Fig. 396

88. Concluding Posture

Movements (continued from fig. 396): Turn both your hands outward, let them separate and descend slowly to the outsides of your thighs with your palms facing downward. Then move your feet together (usually the left foot is drawn near the right), thus returning to the original position—standing at attention. Eyes now look horizontally forward (see figs. 397–400).

Fig. 397

Fig. 398

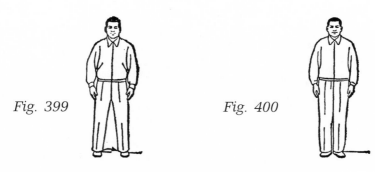

Fig. 399   *Fig. 400*

Notes:

A. In lowering your hands to the outsides of your thighs, you should keep your palms facing downward and your fingers pointing forward as if your were pressing something down.

B. When you move your hands down, exhale slowly and relax your whole body.

C. After finishing your practice, you may do some supplementary exercises or walk around slowly for a while.

CHAPTER VI

T'ai Chi Push Hands

T'ai Chi Push Hands is usually considered to be an important part of the Art of T'ai Chi Ch'uan. It is practiced by two people who are engaged in "joint hand" operations, "pitted" against each other. Adepts think that Push Hands may serve as a touchstone to test whether a practitioner has really grasped the essentials and key points of T'ai Chi Ch'uan— that is to say, when you do Push Hands training, you will find out if you can really make yourself relaxed, if you can draw a clear distinction between "emptiness" and "fullness," if your balance and center of gravity can be consistently maintained in a good state, if the movements of your arms, legs and other parts of the body are harmonized well.

The ingenious designs for Push Hands are imbued with Taoist thoughts and traditional Chinese philosophic theories, such as: "The hard and powerful will disintegrate; the soft and yielding will prevail." "The weak overcome the strong; the gentle overcome the violent." "Make concessions in order to gain advantages." "Apply the antagonist's force back to himself." Besides, Push Hands movements embody the principles of Yin-Yang changes and harmonies. Through Push Hands training you may acquire a better understanding of T'ai Chi Ch'uan exercises.

In the practice of Push Hands, you and your partner alternately use force and yield to force. When you use force to push, it means Yang, hardness, activeness and advance; when you yield to force, it means Yin, softness, passiveness and retreat. Remember, however, Yin and Yang always reside together—there is Yin in Yang, and Yang in Yin; hardness is concealed in softness, and softness in hardness; advance contains retreat, and retreat contains advance.

The most extensively used movements in Push Hands are the four basic ones previously described in the posture of "Grasp the Bird's Tail." They are called "Ward Off," "Roll Back," "Press," and "Push" (see chapters IV, V). It is impossible to do Push Hands exercises without having a good command of them.

Now, let us begin the practical study of Push Hands. As you look at the pictures, imagine yourself to be the person on the left with your partner being the one on the right.

1.   Basic Movements of Push Hands

A.   Preliminaries

Preparatory Stance: You and your partner stand face to face, assume an erect posture which allows every part of the body to enter a natural, easy state. The distance between you and your partner should be kept at the length wherein the faces of your fists can barely touch each other when your arms are raised horizontally (see fig. 1).

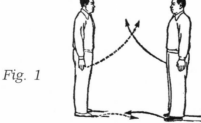

Fig. 1

Starting Stance (continued from fig. 1): Both you and your partner are asked to turn the upper body 45 degrees to the left, and take a step forward with the right foot; the insides of the right feet should face each other with the distance between them being 4–5 inches. At the same time, you raise your right hand forward with arm slightly bent, and your partner does the same. Now the right hands, with their backs facing each other, cross at the wrists. This is generally called "joint hand." The left hands should hang down naturally. The weights should be on both legs (see fig. 2).

Fig. 2

Note: "Joint hand" position has the essence of "ward off," in which your and your partner's force should neither be strong enough to conflict with each other, nor weak enough to appear flabby and powerless.

B.   *Single Push Hands Training*

Movement 1 (continued from fig. 2): You now push forward with your right palm. As you do so, bend your right leg a little, and move your center of gravity slightly forward in order to give your partner a "push" against the right part of his chest with your right palm (see fig. 3). Your partner retracts his right palm to bear your "push" force by means of his "ward off" position. He slightly bends his left leg, shifts his weight backward, turns his upper body right, and uses his right palm to lead yours to his right side to make it fail to touch his chest (see fig. 4).

Fig. 3

Fig. 4

Movement 2: Your partner pushes forward with his right palm immediately after it has led your right palm into failure. His purpose is to give a "push" against the right part of your chest with his right palm (see fig. 5). You, in turn, use the "ward off" position to bear his "push" force. Slightly retract your right arm along with his "push" movement, bend your left leg, shift your weight backward, turn your upper body right, and use your right palm to lead his to your right side to make it fail to touch your chest (see fig. 6).

Fig. 5   Fig. 6

You and your partner may practice the above movements (1 and 2) over and over again in a reciprocating way. You will find that your hands-pushing route assumes a plane circle.

Note: Try to neutralize the opponent's "push" force, instead of resisting it. Do not allow the upper body to unduly lean forward while making a "push." Rotate the waist, hold in the hips, and move the center of gravity back but do not let the upper body lean backward while taking a measure to neutralize the opponent's "push" force. Always keep a little of "ward off" force. Be free to advance and retreat. The right wrists of both partners should always be in contact with each other, like two adhered sliding bearings. The left hands of both partners should move naturally and play a supporting role to the legs and waists.

Movement 3: Return to the preliminary position (see fig. 2). In this movement you intend to give a "push" against your partner's face; therefore, push forward and upward with your right palm, bend your right leg and move your center of gravity slightly forward. Your partner will bear your "push" force by means of the "ward off" motion of his right hand. He will bend his left leg a little, move his weight back, rotate his waist right, and take advantage of your "push" to lead your right palm to the right side of his head. And your intention now ends in failure (see fig. 7).

Fig. 7

Movement 4: Your partner slowly turns his right palm outward, then pushes forward and downward with it, intending to give a "push" at your right rib. You, in turn, use the "ward off" motion of your right hand to bear his "push" force. Yielding to his push, retract your right arm, bend your left leg, move your center of gravity back, and turn your waist to the right, leading his right arm to your right side. His intention now ends in failure (see figs. 8, 9).

Fig. 8

Fig. 9

Movement 5: Turn your right arm into the "push" position and push against your partner's face. Your partner now turns his upper body slightly right, uses the "ward off" motion of his right hand to lead your right hand to the right side of his head, causing your "push" to fail. Immediately after that, he takes up the "push" position and pushes toward your face. You now bend your left leg a little, shift your weight backward, and turn your upper body to the right, leading his right arm away and causing his "push" to fail. Next, turn your right palm outward, push downward and forward with it, aiming at his right rib (see figs. 10, 11, 12).

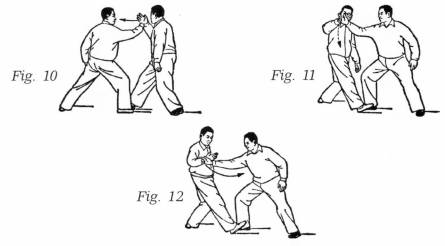

Fig. 10

Fig. 11

Fig. 12

You and your partner may practice Movements 3, 4, and 5 time and time again. You may perform the exercises in varying stances: right hand leading and the right foot in front—left hand leading and the left foot in front—then the right hand leading with the left foot in front—and the left hand leading with the right foot in front. You will find that your hands pushing route approximates a vertical circle.

C. Double Push Hands Training

Movement 1 (continued from fig. 2): After the "joint hand" position (see fig. 2) is formed, you rest your left palm on your partner's right elbow, and he rests his on yours (see fig. 13).

Fig. 13

Movement 2: Turn your right palm outward and rest it on your partner's right wrist, then push forward and downward. Meanwhile, give a "push" on his right elbow in the same direction with your left palm. Your intention is to force his right arm to retreat close to his chest and lose ability to move (see figs. 14, 15).

Fig. 14   *Fig. 15*

Your partner now applies his "ward off" force of both arms to absorbing your "push" force. To achieve this he bends his left leg slightly, shifts his weight backward, rotates his waist right, and leads your "push" to his right side with his right arm (see fig. 16).

Fig. 16

Movement 3: Your partner, immediately after diverting your "push" force, turns his right palm to rest it on your right wrist, and then pushes forward and downward with both his palms (see figs. 17, 18). His intention and movements are just the same as yours. Therefore, deal with him as he dealt with you (see figs. 15, 16).

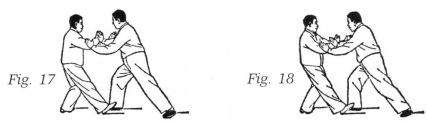

Fig. 17   Fig. 18

You and your partner may practice the above-mentioned movements (including Movements 1, 2, 3) over and over again, in a circulating way, to grasp the techniques. This is usually called "Double Push Hands Plane-Circle Training."

2. Fixed-Step Push Hands

The Preparatory Stance is the same as mentioned under "Preliminaries" of Section 1.

Movement 1: The Starting Stance—the use of "ward off" force (continued from fig. 1): Both you and your partner use the right hands to make contact with each other, forming the "joint hand" position. In the "joint hand" position, you and your partner are actually engaged in using "ward off" force (see fig. 19).

Fig. 19

Movement 2: The use of "roll back" force: yielding to your partner's "ward off" force, you draw back your right arm. Then, turn your right palm outward and let it rest on your partner's right wrist; raise your left palm and let it rest on his right elbow. Meanwhile, taking advantage of your partner's challenge, bend your left leg, hold in your hips, rotate your waist right, and lead his right arm to your right side with both your hands. This denotes a "roll back" motion of yours (see fig. 20).

Fig. 20

Movement 3: The use of "press" force: yielding to your "roll back" motion, your partner slightly bends his right leg and moves his weight a little forward. At the same time, he brings up his left palm and attaches it to the inside of his right arm, then presses against your chest with his right forearm. He intends to divert your "roll back" force and compel both your hands to remain in front of your chest for the time being (see fig. 21).

Fig. 21

Movement 4: The use of "push" force: yielding to his "press" force, you now bend your right leg slightly, hold in your chest and hips, rotate your waist a little left, and push his right arm downward and to the left with both your hands so as to make his "press" end in failure. Immediately after that, you move your right hand to his left elbow and your left hand to his left wrist, then push downward and forward with both palms (see fig. 22).

Fig. 22

Movement 5: Your partner now deals with your "push" by means of his "ward off." As he uses the back of his left hand to bear your left hand, his right hand comes up in a round-about way from the right to rest on your left elbow. Meanwhile, he bends his left leg, shifts his center of gravity backward, and turns his upper body slightly to the left in order that he may "ward off" your "push" with his left arm. Then, he leads your left arm toward his upper left side with both hands, and thus turns his hands into "roll back" movement (see fig. 23).

Fig. 23

Movement 6: With his "roll back" movement, you take your right hand away from his left elbow, and let it attach to the inside of your left elbow, then "press" against his chest with your left forearm. You are now in the "press" position (see figs. 24, 25).

Fig. 24   Fig. 25

Movement 7: Your partner, with your "press" movement, turns his waist to the right, holds in his hips, and turns both his hands from "roll back" movement into "push" movement (see figs. 26, 27).

Fig. 26   Fig. 27

Movement 8: While your partner is pushing forward, your right arm takes up the "ward off" position to cope with his "push." Your left hand comes up in a roundabout way from the left to rest on his right elbow, and your upper body turns to the right. At this time, your "ward off" position turns into the "roll back" position, and his "push" position turns into the "press" position (see fig. 28)

Fig. 28

You and your partner may practice the above-mentioned movements (movements 1–8, figs. 19–28) over and over again, in a circulating way.

Change hands in "Fixed-Step Push Hands":

When your partner presses against your chest with his right arm (as is shown in fig. 21), you lead his left hand to your left side with your left hand instead of pushing his right arm with both your hands. Meanwhile, turn your body slightly to the left, and change your right hand from rolling back his left elbow into the movement of rolling back his left arm (see fig. 29).

Fig. 29

When your partner's left arm is rolled back by you, he bends his front leg, and, along with your "roll back" movement, changes into "press" movement with his left arm (see fig. 30).

Fig. 30

Having neutralized his "press" force, you turn your hands into the "push" position. He now brings his left hand up in a roundabout way from the left and rests it on your right elbow, and then moves his body backward to "roll back" your right arm. You immediately initiate the "push" movement (see fig. 31). Now, both you and your partner have completed the change of hands.

Fig. 31

3. *Moving-Step Push Hands*

A. Three Steps Forward and Two Steps Backward

The Preparatory Stance is the same as mentioned under "Preliminaries" of Section 1.

Starting Stance (continued from fig. 1): You take a step forward with your left foot while your partner does the same with his right foot; his foot is on the outside of yours. You and your partner now raise your respective left hands forward and cross them at the wrists with their backs facing each other, forming the "joint hand" position. Meanwhile, you put your right hand on his left elbow, and he puts his on yours; you take up the "press" position with your left arm, and he assumes the "push" position with both his hands (see fig. 32).

Fig. 32

Movement 1: Your partner shifts his right foot from the outside to the inside of your left foot (this is his first forward step) while he pushes your left arm with both his hands (see fig. 33).

Fig. 33

Movement 2: Take a step back with your left foot (this is your first backward step) and let your right hand meet your partner's over your left elbow. In the meantime, bring your left hand up in a roundabout way from the left and rest it on his right elbow to begin rolling back. Along with your "roll back" movement, your partner takes another step forward (his second forward step) with his left foot which is to alight outside your right foot, preparing to initiate a "press" movement (see fig. 34).

Fig. 34

Movement 3: You back up another step (your second backward step) with your right foot. Meanwhile, lead your partner's right arm with your hands and "roll back" it to your right side with the rightward turning of your body. Following your "roll back" motion, your partner takes a step forward once more (his third forward step) with his right foot which is to alight inside your left foot, and bends his right leg at the knee, keeping his arms in the "press" position. You now slightly bend your right leg, shift your weight a little backward and hold in your hips, turning into "push" position (see figs. 35, 36).

Fig. 35   *Fig. 36*

Movement 4: Following your partner's forward pressing movement, you turn your waist slightly to the left. Simultaneously, shift your left foot from the outside to the inside of your partner's right foot (your first forward step) and push forward with your hands (see fig. 37).

Fig. 37

Movement 5: Along with your forward pushing movement, your partner immediately retreats a step (his first backward step) with his right foot. Meanwhile, he brings his right hand up in a roundabout way from the right and puts it on your left elbow to begin rolling back. Taking advantage of his "roll back," you take another step forward (your second forward step) with your right foot which is to alight outside his left foot (see fig. 38).

Fig. 38

Movement 6: Your partner takes another step back (his second backward step) with his left foot while he rolls back your left arm. With his "roll back" movement, your left foot moves one more step forward (your third forward step) to the inside of his right foot. Now, you turn into the "press" position, and he comes into the "push" position, thus returning to the Starting Stance (shown in fig. 32).

In this sequence of exercises, you and your partner each take three steps forward and two steps backward by turns. When it is your turn to step forward, your hand-arm movement will change from "push" into "press"; when it is your turn to step backward, your hand-arm movement will change from "ward off" into "roll back." During the change from advance to retreat or vice versa, you and your partner should always keep a little of "ward off" force, and do not lose contact with each other. You and your partner may practice this sequence of exercises in endless cycles.

B.　Three Steps Forward and Three Steps Backward

The Preparatory Stance and Starting Stance are just the same as mentioned under "Preliminaries" of Section 1 and shown in figs. 1 and 2.

The method of practice is almost the same as that of *A* except that you are asked to back up three steps (instead of two steps) when it is your turn to step backward, and that both you and your partner begin with right foot forward.

The footwork is as follows: After the "joint hand" position is formed, whoever takes the lead in stepping forward should take the first step with the front foot, and whoever is the first to step backward should retreat the first step with the rear foot. Only in this way can it be possible to take three steps forward and three steps backward.

Movement 1 (continued from fig. 2): Bow your right leg to move your weight forward, initiate a "press" against your partner's chest with your left arm, and let your right hand attach to the inside of your left elbow as support. Your partner holds in his hips and chest to start a "push" with his hands while taking a small step forward (his first forward step) with his right foot. Yielding to his "push" force, you back up a step (your first backward step) with your left foot. After that, he takes another step forward (his second forward step) with his left foot, and you take another step backward (your second backward step) with your right foot. And then, he advances again with his right foot (his third forward step), and you retreat again with your left foot (your third backward step). During the whole process, the hand-arm movements of you and your partner are completely the same as in *A*. Generally speaking, along with the movements of legs, your arms turn from "press," through "ward off" and "roll back," into "push," while your partner's arms turn from "push" into "press" (see figs. 39–43).

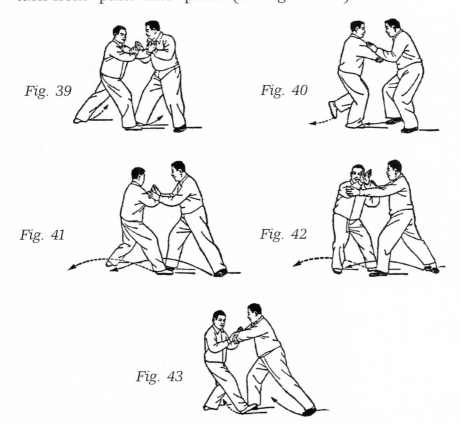

Fig. 39

Fig. 40

Fig. 41

Fig. 42

Fig. 43

Movement 2: Now, it is your turn to advance, and his turn to retreat. The process and movements are the same as mentioned in Movement 1, only you will act the part your partner just did, and he will act the part you just did. You begin with holding in your hips and chest to start a "push" with your hands and lifting up your right foot to step forward; your partner will begin with retreating a step with his left foot (see figs. 44–47).

Fig. 44

Fig. 45

Fig. 46

Fig. 47

C. Flexible Roll Back

The Preparatory Stance and Starting Stance are the same as mentioned under "Preliminaries" of Section 1 and shown in figs. 1 and 2.

Movement 1 (continued from fig. 2): Turn your right hand outward to take a false hold of your partner's right wrist, raise your left hand and put it on his left elbow. As you do so, draw your right foot a half step back to rest beside the left foot, and turn your body slightly to the right to start rolling back. Along with your movements, your partner immediately moves his

left foot a half step forward to the inside of his right foot, and
shifts his weight slightly forward (see fig. 48).

Fig. 48

Movement 2: Following your partner's forward moving, turn
your body right, take a step backward to the right with your
right foot, and let your hands keep on rolling back with your
body's turn, so that he is unable to stand stable on his feet.
Forced by your "roll back" movement, he takes a long step
forward with his left foot again and starts to do "press" movement, but his body is still somewhat off-balance by now (see
fig. 49).

Fig. 49

Movement 3: Along with your continuous rolling back, your
partner steps forward again with his right foot which is to
alight inside your left foot, and moves his weight slightly
forward onto his right leg. Meanwhile, he puts his left hand
on the inside of his right arm and initiates a "press" against
your chest (see fig. 50).

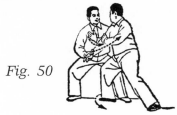

Fig. 50

Movement 4: As a reaction to his "press" movement, you immediately hold in your hips, turn your waist to the left, shift your weight onto your right leg, and change your hands from rolling back into pushing. At the same time, lift your left foot and shift it quickly from the outside to the inside of his right foot (see fig. 51).

Fig. 51

Movement 5: Following your pushing, your partner uses the back of his left hand to cope with your left hand, and brings his right hand up to rest on your left elbow. While doing so, he draws his right foot a half step back to the inside of his left foot, shifts his weight slightly to the left, and turns his hands from pressing into rolling back. You, now, allow your left leg to bend a little forward, shifting your weight slightly to the front (see fig. 52).

Fig. 52

Movement 6: Your partner turns his body to the left, takes a step backward to the left with his left foot, and continues doing "roll back" with both his hands (his left hand taking a false hold of your left wrist, and his right hand resting on your left elbow). Making use of his "roll back" force, you take a stride forward with your right foot and move your weight forward onto your right leg (see fig. 53).

Fig. 53

Movement 7: Following your partner's continuous rolling back, you take one more step forward with your left foot which is to alight inside his right foot, and shift your weight slightly forward onto your left leg. As you do so, put your right hand on the inside of your left arm and start a "press" against his chest (see fig. 54).

Fig. 54

In the above sequence of actions, you and your partner take turns to advance once and retreat once. This is called a "round." Now, your partner may advance again with his right foot and turn his hands from rolling back into pushing (see fig. 55), while you may retreat again with your left leg and change your hands from pressing into rolling back (see fig. 56). This can be repeated round after round, without limit.

Fig. 55

Fig. 56

Change hands in "Flexible Roll Back":

As your partner makes a "push" on you with his shoulder, your right hand turns into an open palm and directly pounces at his face. This is called a "pouncing palm" (see fig. 57). Reacting to this, he raises his right hand in front of his face to meet yours and holds it by the wrist. Meanwhile, he puts his left hand on your right elbow, turns his body to the right, draws his right foot back to the inside of his left foot, and, along with his body's turning, changes his hands from pressing into rolling back (see figs. 58, 59). Forced by his "roll back" movement, you shift your weight slightly forward and take a step forward with your right foot which is to alight in front of his feet (see fig. 59).

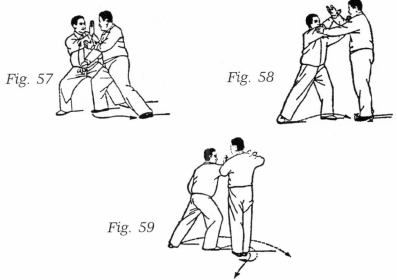

Fig. 57

Fig. 58

Fig. 59

Movement 8: Your partner turns his body further to the right and backs up a step again with his right foot while his hands keep on rolling back. Led by his "roll back" movement, you take a long step forward with your left foot, shift your weight slightly forward, and then take another step forward with your right foot which is to alight inside his left foot. Meanwhile, put your left hand on the inside of your right arm, and begin to "press" towards his chest with both your arms (see fig. 60).

Fig. 60

The footwork and process are roughly the same as in the former sequence of Flexible Roll Back movements. Only in the former case, you "roll back" your partner's right arm while he "rolls back" your left arm, and the change of your parts is achieved by taking a quick step forward and turning hands from rolling back into pushing to neutralize the opponent's "press" force. In the present case, however, each of you "rolls back" the other's right arm, and changes part by pouncing at the other's face with right palm.

If you "push" your partner with your shoulder, he will allow his left palm to pounce at your face (see fig. 61), and you should use your left hand to cope with his left arm. Meanwhile, turn your body to the left to start rolling back (see fig. 62). Along with your "roll back," he steps forward with his right foot and leans his left arm towards your chest (see figs. 63, 64). After this, each of you can use your left palm to pounce at the other's face, and will "roll back" the other's left arm.

Fig. 61

Fig. 62

Fig. 63

Fig. 64

To learn Push Hands well, you must begin with the "Single Push Hands Training," skillfully advancing to "Double Push Hands," then to "Fixed-Step Push Hands," and then to "Moving-Step Push Hands." Proceed in an orderly way, step by step; never be greedy to grasp all in one or two sessions. Practice calmly, slowly.

Index

Zhang Fuxing was born in Shaanxi, China, in 1921. A professor of translation and Honorary Member of the Council of Shaanxi Translators Association, he taught translation courses at Xian Foreign Languages University for many years. There he also served as director of the Translation Teaching and Research Section.

He has published several books, including *Allusive English Idioms, Lectures on Chinese-English Translation* (co-author) and *A Dictionary of English Proverbs with Explanations in both English and Chinese* (co-editor). His essays on translation theory and technique have been published in magazines, such as *Chinese Translator's Journal*, and *Foreign Languages Teaching and Studying*. His translations (from English into Chinese) include works by Dr. Eugene A. Nida and Arthur Conan Doyle.

Zhang Fuxing's lifelong hobby is T'ai Chi Ch'uan. He has studied and practiced this ancient fitness art for over forty years. He has always hoped to share its great benefit with others. *Handbook of T'ai Chi Ch'uan Exercises* is the result of that hope.